The Cosmics
... and the
Origins of Consciousness

The Cosmics

... and the Origins of Consciousness

Gene L Warner

BoysMind Books
Grand Haven, Michigan USA

Copyright © 2014 by Gene L Warner

Grand Haven, Michigan 49417 USA

All rights reserved under International and Pan-American Copyright Conventions.

Published in the United States by

BoysMind Books

www.boysmindbooks.com

3 5 7 9 0 8 6 4 2

Publishers Cataloging in Publication Data

Warner, Gene L.

The Cosmics ... and the Origins of Consciousness

p. cm.

First Edition — July 2014

Description: We mortals are surrounded by an invisible realm of cosmic entities, the mysterious source of transcendent wisdom and conscience that since the beginning of time man has called his gods, or his god. Whether we're aware of it or not, each of us has a cosmic companion that is always present and ready to guide us through life, from cradle to grave.

ISBN: 978-0-9797896-6-3

1. Theosophy and spiritualism. 2. Spirits—invisible world. 3. Guides (Spiritualism). I. Warner, Gene L. II. Title.

BF1275.T5 2014

110.W244 2014

LCCN: 2014944871

In Memory of
"Little Willie"

Contents

Preface i
Introduction iv
1   Bill 1
2   Grand Haven Again 8
3   Little Willie 12
4   Patricide Averted 15
5   Of Things Not Seen 22
6   A Moment of Clarity 28
7   A Complex Miracle 36
8   The Second Apparition 48
9   A Final Appearance 54
10 Forsaken 59
11 But What About Bill? 63
12 Belief In Things Not Seen 68
13 The Nature of the Invisibles 80
14 The Origin of Mind 84
15 From Mind to Madness 88
16 The Mystery of Human Wickedness ... 93
17 The Spirits' Role in Your Life 99
18 Still, Small Voices 105
19 Living with the Cosmics 109

Preface

In dealing with books written about incorporeal things, one very often encounters exotic words with nebulous meanings, used by authors who are attempting to discuss incomprehensively obscure concepts. You might have plodded on through such texts in a futile quest for understanding, only to reach the last page without much reward for your effort.

There are a couple of reasons why this happens.

I've always suspected that if someone isn't able to express themselves clearly, it's usually because no matter how earnest and well intentioned they might be, they don't really know what they're talking about. Just as experts are often able to make complex things look simple, non-experts are apt to make things seem unnecessarily complicated.

But it's also true that regardless of how much one might know about the cosmics and their realm, the nature of those entities and the place where they abide is profoundly unlike anything we know about and ordinarily experience during our existence as physical beings living in our physical domain.

It is said that language is the tool that enables thought; that when thinking we are actually having a conversation with ourselves. Our vocabulary develops through our encounters with each other in the domain we occupy. Therefore, not much of it is useful in thinking about entities and domains that are utterly unlike anything we have ever known. We sometimes have encounters with these other entities and domains, and when we do, the communications are quite clear, and it all seems to make perfect sense. But when attempting to relate such experiences to others, we find ourselves literally *at a loss for words*.

By way of definitions...

I use the word *cosmic* as a noun, thus coining a new use of the word to provide a simplified means of referring to entities that are *supernatural* (meaning above and beyond what is explainable by natural laws or phenomena) and *incorporeal* (meaning not physical, material or tangible.) I had originally settled on the word *spirit*, but was uncomfortable with that because of its various extraneous connotations. Cosmic comes from a Greek word *kosmos* which originally referred to things of this world, but later on took on a broader scope relating to things of the universe. That seemed especially appropriate, since the entities I wish to talk about are as much a part of this world as a part of the universe. Thus, instead of using Carl Jung's term "spirit guide," I'll use *cosmic companion*. I'll call an individual such entity a *cosmic*; *cosmics* referring to more than one of them, or the class of such entities in general.

I use the words *realm*, or *domain*, interchangeably in referring to the invisible sphere in which these entities abide. This is not meant as a reference to some place different from the space in the universe that we physically occupy. It might be different in some cases, but can also be in our midst and invisible to us, just as the molecules of the air that we breathe are not visible.

Human beings are inventers of religions, almost all of which have supernatural entities which abide in other realms. This has happened all around the world and in every culture because people have always correctly sensed the presence of the cosmics, and recognized that they sometimes choose to intervene in human affairs.

In man's ignorance, the cosmics have more often than not been reduced to concepts that are familiar; identifiable entities, with a hierarchical social structure, each one having a name and occupying a specific realm, usually somewhere in the heavens, or under the ground. As such notions are invented and developed through the ages by successive generations they accumulate increasingly elaborate stories, traditions, dogmas, rituals, and sacraments. Eventually they become formally and firmly established as organized religions, thus inheriting an aura of credibility and authority.

It is therefore impossible to avoid bumping into these religions when writing about the cosmics. Some of what I have written supports certain beliefs; in other cases, it does not. Be that as it may, this is not a book about religion. It is not my purpose to promote any particular religious philosophy, or to critique it.

Introduction

I've quit referring to them as "spirit friends." That was always just a euphemism of sorts, since I never really thought that they were *friends*, at least not in the usual sense. It also seemed somewhat presumptive, as if I actually thought, or was trying to suggest, that I had some special standing with such mystical entities.

I don't, and I wasn't.

In the beginning it was always just a single *presence* of some sort; a presence that was quite real, but ineffable, although it always seemed like a companionate male. I eventually began to think of *him* as my *cosmic companion*. I got that idea from reading about Carl Jung's experience with what he called his *spirit guide*, whom he called "Philemon." I had already sensed by then that there was, and had always been, a companion of some sort journeying through life with me; perhaps what people colloquially refer to as a guardian angel. But it was more than that; more than just an invisible hand that kept me out of harms way now and then. It was also *conscience*, and an ethereal sort of consultant that could be relied upon to help throttle impulsiveness and promote better judgment. That's the way it apparently is for most people who have such encounters; a one-on-one sort of relationship.

But the time came for that companion to be freed of the responsibility of holding hands with me, and he departed. His departure was amicable; he was apparently able to leave because I had become old enough, experienced enough, and near enough to the end of my journey through this life to be able to go the rest of the way successfully, or at least uneventfully, on my own. But after his departure, others from his realm randomly appeared, and I then realized that they had been around all the time.

After first sensing that I had an invisible partner in life, that he was not merely an imaginary friend, that he came from some other realm where there were many others like him, belief proved fickle. In our culture, such beliefs are generally disparaged as the province of charlatans, fools and the insane, and are therefore best kept to oneself. Nobody wants to be considered different than everyone else. The pressure to conform that arises from our need to feel accepted and well thought of is cogent and cannot be ignored.

So alone with my secret ideas, and cautious about being found out, there were always moments of doubt. Then I would have another experience that once again removed all doubt. As time dimmed the vision of that experience, doubt would gradually return yet again; were those previous experiences real, or delusional; perhaps caused by some sort of chemical disturbance in my brain? But then something else would happen, occurring during a time when I was fully conscious and feeling perfectly normal. That made it difficult, once again, to not believe.

Common sense finally prevailed and removed the doubts once and for all. Once again, it was something Carl Jung had once said...

"Nobody who has not had such experiences can believe that they are real, and nobody who has, cannot not believe."

And so, I have come to *know* without doubt that we live in the midst of a realm of incorporeal beings that have the ability to intervene, or meddle, in our affairs whenever they feel so inclined. I suspect that we mortals have sensed this from the very beginning, mistakenly calling them our gods, or our god.

1
Bill

When I was about four years old, or whatever the age is when a little boy begins to remember things, I had a playmate named Bill. I don't remember ever wondering where Bill came from; he just seemed to appear whenever I was lonely and needed a playmate. He was only *my* friend; nobody else's.

We, my mother, older sister and I, lived at 623 West 8th Street in Traverse City, a small town back then lying in the crook between the little finger and the ring finger on the Michigan mitten. It was probably during the year 1944. My father, a Coast Guard Chief, was in the war so he was never home. I don't remember ever seeing him until after WW-II ended and he finally came home towards the end of the summer in 1946. I was just then going on six years old.

There were other kids in our little close knit Traverse City neighborhood but, except for three much older boys, they were all girls.

Hal Goss, was one of the older boys; a few years older than my older sister and her friends, so probably about ten. He lived in a little house across the alley behind ours with his parents and little sister Reva, a skinny little blonde girl. Reva and I sometimes played together upstairs in the attic of her house, where there were cartons full of order pads like restaurant waitresses use. I don't know why they were there, but she and I would spend our time together quietly filling out orders, complete with carbon copies. Her big brother ultimately shot my stubborn big sister through the wrist with an arrow when she refused to move away from a target that he'd fastened to a stack of hay bales. I don't remember ever being able to play with Reva again after that.

The other two were the Steiger boys who lived with their mother at the end of the block. We didn't really know them because they were older teenagers, and wild. All I remember about them is that they lived with their single mother, were bad boys, that they got drunk together one night and laughingly puked out their bedroom window. We snuck over there the next morning to see where the vomit had drizzled down the outside of their house.

My sister was four years older than me. The Kimmit family, who lived on the west side of our little house, had two daughters about her age, as did the Schulte family on the other side. Besides that, she went to Central School just down the street, so she had lots of friends and playmates. Since I had none, she was usually expected to include me as she and her friends played together. She hated me for it. She and her friends would chant "Tag-along, tag-along! Go home, tag-along!" And I would cry. Then they would yell "Cry-baby cripsie, sucks his mamma's titsie!" My sister would tell me, "I hate you! We all hate you!" and her friends would say that I was going to turn into a sissy boy because I played with girls all the time.

But then Bill came along. I don't remember exactly when he started to come around, but even if I was outdoors with my sister and her friends because my mother was making her watch over me, I wasn't really that much of a bother anymore. Bill and I would find our own things to do, and we'd play by ourselves. Much of the time we wouldn't even go outdoors, and would just play quietly by ourselves in the living room of our little house. So my sister and her friends were no longer always stuck with me *tagging along*.

Bill and I did a lot of talking. To anyone listening, it was a one sided conversation, like listening to someone talking on the telephone. Nobody could hear Bill's side of it but me.

My fifth year in life might well have been my last.

I had been enrolled in school early, still only four years old when I entered Central School's Kindergarten in the fall of 1945. I wasn't prepared for that. Most of the time I had no idea what was going on or what I was supposed to be doing. I didn't even understand the concept of *recess*. When the teacher, Miss Foot, would send us outside to play on the playground for recess, I'd go home. I remember Kindergarten as a very confusing and stressful ordeal.

But at least there were other boys at school, and I did finally get a real boy for a playmate. His name was, coincidentally (or perhaps not so coincidentally) "Bill;" William Breithaupt. "Billy Bright-up," as I called him, was exactly one year older than me. He lived far away, on the other end of town, but was occasionally left in the care of his grandmother, who lived closer to our neighborhood, and then sometimes we'd get to play together away from school. Sometimes I'd be taken to his grandma's house, and sometimes Billy would come to our house.

To the west of our Eighth Street home in Traverse City, across Division Avenue, a hundred yards down the grassy hill and across what was then an open field, was a creek; known today, (ironically) as *Kid's Creek*, but back then we called it the Boardman Creek, probably because it didn't really have a name in those days, but flowed into the Boardman River.

On the other side of the creek was a place where kids could find clay. My sister and her friends often went over there to get some, which they'd bring home and turn into dolls, dishes, and various other little things. Naturally, I'd tag along on those expeditions. Part of the big field, including the creek, was fenced off with a woven wire fence, and that's how we'd get across the creek to the other side; by climbing onto the fence and traversing sideways above the water, side-step by side-step—a rather scary proposition for me as a little boy.

On a late spring day in 1946, Billy Brightup came over to our house to play. While his grandma and my mother went shopping together, we were left in the care of a young babysitter. I suppose it was my idea to show my best friend the creek, how we made the dangerous crossing on the wire fence, and the clay beds on the other side. Without bothering the inattentive young babysitter, the two of us, just five and six years old, quietly slipped away across the busy Division Avenue and down the hill to Boardman Creek.

The winter snowmelt and the spring rains had left the field marshy in spots, and the creek was running much higher than it did in the summertime. During the summer months the water was shallow, clear and warm, flowing gently by under the fence. Falling off the fence while crossing the creek would have been "dangerous" only because of a parent's likely response when their child came home soaked and covered with mud. So it was really just part of the adventure for my sister and her friends to pretend that it was a dangerous crossing, but being much younger, I'd never caught on to that. I took them at their word, and always felt like it was a frightening undertaking, usually had to be coaxed, and was always much relieved upon safely reaching the other side.

But now, in the springtime, it was different. The water was much deeper, much darker, much colder, and was flowing by swiftly. Seeing that, I wasn't sure about crossing over to the other side on the fence anymore.

And then came the flower.

Floating rapidly along on the surface in the middle of the creek was a pretty, white blossom. I thought of my teacher, Miss. Foot, and how pleased she might be were I to present her with that pretty flower. I ran to find a long stick, hoping to fish it over to the edge so I could reach down and get it, but the longest stick I could find on such short notice was not quite long enough. Squatting on the edge of the embankment and reaching out as far as I could, I lost my balance and fell into the rushing water.

Having been so well conditioned by my sister and her friends to fear this very situation, I was overcome with fright. Even to this day I can remember what it felt like to be tumbling over and over in the darkness beneath the surface of that cold, rushing water.

It seemed like a long time, but obviously must have been only a few moments before my hand somehow found a singular large root growing out of the side of the bank, just below the surface of the water. Thanks to that, I was able to get my head above water and hold on for dear life. The bank was too high for me to be able to climb out, so that was all I could do; just hold on. I didn't see Billy anywhere so assumed that, knowing that we had now gotten into trouble, he had run away. So I just held on, shivering and crying as the cold and uncaring waters of the Boardman Creek rushed heedlessly by.

But my real friend Billy hadn't really run off. He had scurried back to our house to raise the alarm, and it wasn't very long before I saw the faces of several concerned adults appear over the edge of the bank above me. I was saved!

Not much was ever made of this episode. People were more practical and unflappable about such things then, and probably dismissed it saying things like, "Oh, well; boys will be boys." or "All's well that ends well."

But it did scar me for life; from that day on I'd always be afraid of the water, never learning to swim until finally teaching myself on the beach at Biloxi, Mississippi. I was in the U.S. Air Force, twenty-one years old, and discovered that Biloxi's manmade beach in the Gulf of Mexico provided about a hundred yards of calm, shallow water, with few other beach goers on hand to witness my clumsy thrashing around while I was trying to learn how to at least float and dog paddle. So I succeeded in teaching myself how to swim, but I've never gotten over my fear of deep water and the impulse to panic at the slightest hint of alarm.

Thinking back to that terrible day in the Boardman Creek, I have to wonder how many "Bills" were there with me. As I was thrashing around in a panic, tumbling over and over under the water, was it the invisible Bill who took my hand in his and placed it on that one, single large root that saved my life?

———

Towards the end of the summer that year, when my dad finally came home from the war, it was in a big, navy gray Coast Guard truck. They packed up all our stuff and loaded it onto that big gray military truck, and took it all down to Grand Haven. We moved to Grand Haven because after the war my dad was transferred to the Life Saving Station there.

As clearly as I can remember, I never seemed to notice that Bill, my imaginary friend Bill, did not come along, and I never saw him again—at least not for a long, long time after that.

2
Grand Haven Again

I didn't know it then, but I had lived in Grand Haven before. Not long after I was born on South Manitou Island, most of the Coast Guardsmen in the Great Lakes area were called to sea for convoy escort duty. My dad's married sister Lenore lived in Grand Haven, and he had decided that we'd be better off living near her and her family, rather than to remain out on the island near his parents and other relatives, but otherwise isolated during the long winter months. We didn't stay long. I was baptized in Grand Haven's founding church, the First Presbyterian Church, on Sunday, the 13th day of June in 1943. Soon after that, against my dad's wishes and much to his dismay, my mother moved back up north, to the little house on West 8th Street in Traverse City.

The Coast Guard Station at Grand Haven was located on "north shore," as it was called, just across the Grand River from the city. There wasn't much else on north shore back then. We moved into one of the three little houses right next to the station, and that's where we lived for the next year or so.

Except for some other Coast Guardsmen, there were no neighbors. From the Grand River channel all the way down the beach to the north, to the place where North Shore

Road, the road to town, turned inland, it was all just barren sand dunes. There were only three houses along that stretch of beach, which we'd sometimes walk with a young sailor who was doing shore patrol; one deserted and "haunted," one boarded up, and finally one that we figured must be the home of some rich people; an elaborate cottage made of brick and stone and overlooking Lake Michigan from atop one of the low dunes.

The only other house was on the opposite side of North Shore Road about half way between the Station and the curve; a small bungalow with a family named the Murphys. They had one boy and three girls, but they were Catholic so didn't go to our school. Their parents were tavern owners, so worked long hours, and the Murphy kids lived too far away to play with anyway.

So my sister and I were then in the same boat. Neither of us had any friends or playmates on north shore. Under those circumstances, we briefly became companions.

And so life went on, but not for the better. When not on duty our dad drank beer, one bottle after another, and as he became increasingly inebriated, he also became progressively more irritable and mean.

About a year later, we moved from there across the channel into what had, during the war, been a Coast Guard Training Camp. A couple years later we moved into town. Another sister had been born, and two brothers. Our family became increasingly dysfunctional with episodes of domestic violence bursting out more and more often. The assaults and beatings were occasionally dangerously vicious, and life became increasingly confused, insecure and sad.

It was the late 1940s and 1950s; a time when things were going well for most working class families. People respected privacy, keeping their noses out of other people's business and their problems to themselves. It was a time when *Life With Father* had become the archetypical image of family; a time during the early development of television when strict codes of decency restricted broadcasters to air dramas and situation comedies depicting only the most wholesome behavior.

Our family was nothing like that.

Our family was a vulgar, hateful and dangerous place; a situation that I was profoundly self conscious of, and ashamed of. Today I realize that none of that was ever my fault; that I'd simply had the bad luck of having been born to two terribly neurotic people who should never have married each other. But back then I was a child, and didn't know that. Nor did I know that I was equally wrong in thinking that our troubled family was unique. I believed that I was part of our family, and therefore a part of everything that was wrong with it. I believed that if other people knew what went on in our house, we would be judged *bad people*, not worthy of anybody's respect and friendship.

For my own sake, I therefore became secretive. I became quiet, standoffish, and eventually a loner. By the time I graduated from high school and left home, I had developed what the psychologists call "AvPD"—*Avoidant Personality Disorder*. I avoided close personal relationships, keeping everyone at arm's length for fear that they would discover what sort of people I was really from and what I was really like, and would then realize that I was not worthy of their friendship. That was, of course, a dumb strategy, since it virtually guaranteed the outcome that it was devised to prevent; I wound up with no friends anyway!

Ironically, I'd come full circle over the fourteen years between ages four and eighteen: once again, I had no friends. I was a loner. And I remained that way for the next eighteen years—alone.

Or so I thought.

3
Little Willie

Almost every year during our times of troubles in the late 1940s and early 1950s, after the going had gotten really rough, always during the heat of the summer months, my mother would flee north for safety with us children, back to Port Oneida; the place where she was born. My older sister and I would usually stay with our uncle and aunt on the home place, the Kelderhouse farm, while she and the other three children would move in with another aunt and uncle who lived in a cozy little cottage alongside Fisher Lake, a few miles away.

My older sister and I had stayed on the farm many times before, beginning as far back as I could remember ... in happy days before the end of WW-II and the return of our father. Uncle Rolland and Aunt Aggie actually liked each other, enjoyed each other, and worked together harmoniously. Unlike our home, the farm was a peaceful, pleasant and fun place. What was actually an estrangement, and probably a regular nuisance to my mother's people up north, seemed like a vacation to us, and we'd soon forget about the dark and fearful goings on in Grand Haven.

Just to the south of the farmhouse was the Kelderhouse cemetery, a one-acre plot with the graves of family members going back to the original settlers from Germany, as well as those of friends and neighbors from nearby farms in the Port Oneida farming community. In the middle of the cemetery was a well with an old cast iron pitcher pump. Pumping water up by hand from somewhere underground was intriguing, and just for the fun of doing it, my sister and I frequently took it upon ourselves to water the flowers on all of the graves.

Grandma Kelderhouse had nine children, only four of whom lived well into adulthood. The other five were all laid to rest in the little Kelderhouse cemetery, most of them in a rectangular family plot enclosed within a low curb-like cement border. I was always drawn to one of these graves in particular, the one with a small white alabaster headstone that said "WILLIE" across its curved top edge.

William Kelderhouse Jr., "Little Willie," died in the nearby farmhouse on January 8, 1899. He had lived only one year and eight months. I don't really know why his life was cut so short, but my guess is that it was influenza; there was a world wide epidemic of Russian Flu back then, which also swept through Michigan's northern counties, peaking in January of 1899.

Almost all of the dear departed souls who rested eternally around Willie's grave in that cemetery were his relatives. They were also mine, but it was Willie's grave that I was always drawn to. And even today as I look at pictures of his headstone, which has long since disappeared either at the hands of vandals, or the natural forces of the elements, I get a hollow feeling in my chest, perhaps better described as a *yearning*.

Many years would pass between the time that I, as a little boy, would wander around that old country graveyard toting a heavy watering can, often sitting down for a while to rest in the shade next to Willie's little headstone, and the time in my adult life when I finally realized what the connection was between me and that other little boy, actually my uncle, and why it had meant so much to me over all those years.

When I was a lonely little boy, was it Willie who came to be my friend and companion, my "Bill?" As I grew up, was it he who remained by my side? As I reflect back on the bad times of my later boyhood, I now think about all the awful things that could have been; about all the times that my silly or hateful impulses were throttled, about all the times when I was nudged towards the better path and away from courses leading to dead ends or degradation—but then also about the unlikely assortment of people who mysteriously came into my life to teach me that I was worth the attention that they lavished on me. How much of that was Willie's doing?

I was always too busy lamenting my situation and feeling sorry for myself to realize that I was never struggling through my troubled childhood alone; that "Bill," *Little Willie*, was always there with me.

Or, at least, that's what I came to believe.

4
Patricide Averted

Because he was absent during the earliest of my formative years, my dad eventually concluded that I had been raised under the influence of my mother's family, and had become one of those "goddamned Kelderhouses"—his words. We never had much of a relationship to begin with. After a couple of his beatings as a little boy, I was scared to death of him, and did my best to keep out of his way. But as I grew into my adolescent years, he became pointedly antagonistic, always making it plain that he didn't like me, and the feeling was mutual.

When I was fifteen, our relationship hit its all time low.

Our mother, who had always been a homemaker after marrying, had gotten a job working as a white uniformed waitress at the local Country Club. She justified that by claiming that the family needed the additional income, although by that time our dad had retired from the Coast Guard, and had taken a good paying job as a maintenance engineer at the local piano factory. In addition to that paycheck, he was receiving his monthly retirement check from the U.S. Government so, in retrospect, their actual need for additional income seems doubtful. Her real motive was more likely to get out of the house and away from him.

This only seemed to make things worse, with him getting into the habit of stewing over things during her absence, working himself up into a hateful mood while downing a couple of six-packs of *Blatz* beer, and conjuring up plans for spitefully dealing with her when she returned home. This eventually became a routine. On her return there'd be a heated argument with him pushing her around, slapping and choking her while she cried and pleaded. He'd utter the most vulgar accusations, calling her a whore and a slut, before eventually kicking her out of the house and locking the doors.

By this time my older sister had left, having decided to emancipate herself as soon as she turned sixteen years old, and after having received the most severe beating ever from our father. That left the four of us younger children, me at fifteen, my younger sister who was ten, and my two younger brothers who were just eight and six. It was a Saturday, and the day had begun as usual, with the sound of a "church key" punching through the top of a beer can around ten o'clock in the morning. Our mother had gone to work early in the afternoon, as she usually did on Saturdays, and the stewing began not long thereafter.

By seven o'clock or seven-thirty my drunken dad had the four of us kids sitting on the couch, lined up in order from oldest to youngest, with him sitting opposite in what was known as "his chair." With his Western Field 16-guage shotgun propped up along one side of it, and his Winchester

30-30 deer rifle on the other side, he promised, "There's gonna' be bloodshed in this goddamned house tonight!"

Forbidden to move, we sat there … and we sat there … and we sat there in the living room, quietly waiting as the brass Coast Guard clock on the wall in the dining room ticked away the hours, striking out the ship's bells every thirty minutes, the fear and foreboding building as we silently waited for whatever the outcome of this episode was going to be.

Not long after "four bells," ten o'clock, we finally heard a car stop in front of the house … the car door close … the steps on the front porch as the car that she'd come in drove away … the doorknob turn and the door tried … but found locked. Dad then got up, almost nonchalantly, went to the door, opened it and yanked her violently into the house. This time he didn't waste many words, or perhaps it only seems that way in my muddled memory. He soon had her pinned against the wall with his left hand at her throat, and socking her in the face with his right, shouting the most vulgar accusations. "You're nothing but a goddamned whore … you goddamned, goddamned …" so angry that he was actually sputtering and at a loss for words. Perhaps luckily, he'd become so absorbed in his angry fit that he forgot about the guns. Twisting her arm behind her back, he opened the front door and pushed her out of the house, shouting an admonition to "go peddle your ass somewhere else, you goddamned slut; you don't live here anymore!"

Having just suffered one of the more intensive beatings, she fled.

Within a few minutes, for whatever reason, whether he feared that she was leaving for good, or going to the police, or who knows what, he went into the kitchen, grabbed his car keys off the hook where they were always hung above the kitchen sink, then hurried out and drove off in his car to find her.

All this was the last straw for me. I bounded upstairs, grabbed my J.C. Higgins 12-guage, loaded it and hurried back down to pursue him. As I ran out the front door my little sister screamed, "Don't leave us here alone! Where are you going?" My answer was, "Don't worry; I'm gonna kill him!" and with that I was outside and hurrying around the block in search of our white over blue Chevy Deluxe coupe.

I didn't have far to look. As I approached Fulton Street, only one block from our house, I saw him coming. I stood next to a big elm tree, raised my gun and leveled it at the oncoming car with him in my sights and my finger on the trigger. He was coming towards me slowly, apparently searching for our mother along the darkened sidewalks of that moonless night, and he was coming closer ... and closer ... and closer ...

And then he passed by.

I slumped down at the bottom of the big tree, sitting there with my shotgun, crying like a child and hating myself for not having had the courage to shoot my father and put an end to everyone's misery. I really didn't understand what had happened. When I left the house, I had every intention of killing the sonofabitch, and then when the time came, when I had a clear shot and could have easily blown his head off, I just stood there letting the car pass by!

The next thing I did was stranger yet.

The local police station was just up the 5th Street hill, only a block and a half away. I walked up the hill, entered the station, and breathing heavily with nervous excitement, plopped my loaded 12-guage down on the desk sergeant's counter. Struggling to hold back the tears, I managed to choke out, "You'd better take this, because if I ever find my dad I'm going to kill him!"

Noticing that the desk sergeant was visibly shaken, I suddenly woke up to the potential seriousness of the scene, and to the fact that my mother was also there, apparently having fled to the police for protection and to urge them to rescue us kids from her berserk husband.

Thinking back on this episode a few days later, I was able to rationalize that my intention was only to make a scene that would impress people with the seriousness of the situation. It did, in fact, have that effect, but that wasn't really true. By that time I had come to realize that had I succeeded in killing our father, it would have been the end of his life, for sure; but it would also have been the end of mine, and a permanent scar on the souls of everyone else in the family. I wasn't proud of that. In my heart of hearts, I also really felt that I had chickened out when the chips were down, that I was just a coward, "a little man acting too big for his britches," just like my dad had so often said. I wasn't proud of that either. And so I came up with the idea that I'd never really intended him any serious harm, and did my best to teach myself to believe it.

I remember this all quite clearly, even after all these years, including the moment of truth, when while my mind was instructing my right index finger to squeeze, something else was gently lifting it off of the trigger. I remember wondering in the moments immediately following what in the hell had come over me, damning myself for not firing, and then crying so bitterly because I had failed.

It wouldn't be until decades later that I would finally realize what happened that night; that my friend Bill had been there with me, intervening to stop me from impulsively committing what would have certainly been a grievous mistake.

Quite beside the fact that I would have become a teenage murderer, spending the best years of the rest of my life in prison while also having left the rest of the family with indelible scars, I would also come to realize, many years later, that I really never knew what was going on between my parents.

As a child, I could easily observe my dad's drunkenness, anger, his physical meanness and violent behavior, but I was not then psychologically astute enough to see my mother's role in their turbulent relationship. As a remnant of her troubled upbringing, she grew up with a need to be seen as the Cinderella of her family; the victim, the martyr. She covertly invited the abuse in order to achieve validation, and she knew just exactly how to push our dad's buttons in order to instigate it.

Worse yet, after studying our family history and putting together certain facts, I finally came to the conclusion that my older sister was more likely my half-sister and half-cousin, having been fathered by my dad's younger brother, and that my younger sister was more than likely also a half-sister, having been fathered by a foreman at Berwood Products, a small company in Traverse City where our mother had worked very briefly during the war years helping manufacture religious plaques and knick-knacks. Hence Dad's vague, but increasingly bold allegations about her infidelity. And hence her need, probably subconsciously, to even up the score by proving to him that he was just as unworthy of her respect and love as she felt she was of his.

Such facts are not hidden from the cosmics.

5
Of Things Not Seen

In spite of his being thirty years older than I was, my dad was hardly any more psychologically discerning than I was as a boy. He was actually a simple man, a what-you-see-is-what-you-get sort of person with no secrets. He always sensed that our mother was doing things to press his buttons, but he was never able to say exactly how she did it without it sounding extremely childish.

After the shotgun incident, the Presbyterian minister came over to our house a few times for counseling sessions, and while eavesdropping one evening, I heard my dad utter, "Well, now you've heard one side of it, but you don't know anything about the other part." Unhappily for him, of course, he wasn't able to communicate in any coherent way what her part of it was. And at the time I was thinking, "What part!?!"—it seeming plain enough to see who was in the wrong, and it was *all him.*

Dad was also a proud man. He suspected that my younger sister was not his, and he sometimes accused my mother of that, but only in the very vaguest terms. If he ever suspected that my older sister was actually his brother's child—that he had been set up after his brother refused to marry our mother because he also had another girl pregnant at the same time—he never said or did anything to suggest that he did. Even had he suspected that, his pride would have never permitted him to acknowledge it.

The violent part of their relationship ended soon after that incident. It wasn't because of my attention-getting drama, his having spent that night sobering up and cooling off in a jail cell, or the minister's counseling. It was because one afternoon my mother decided to fight back. They were having one of their all too familiar Sunday afternoon rows in the kitchen, and as he began his usual maneuver, using his left hand on her neck to pin her against the wall and his right to hold a knife to her throat, she grabbed a nearby spider, a heavy cast iron skillet, and swinging it with all her strength, whacked him soundly on the left side of his head.

It apparently didn't do much damage, since he simply dropped his hands and backed off with a silly, surprised look on his face that seemed to suggest a feeling that she'd just quite unexpectedly violated the rules of the game. Perhaps he'd always just been a bully, and that's all it would have ever taken to end the physical abuse. At any rate, he never again laid a hand on her as far as I ever knew.

This didn't mean that our relationship, his and mine, got any better. Quite to the contrary, we spent most of the remaining three years before I finally left home hating each other. I was never openly defiant or overtly disrespectful towards him, not because I was trying to be nice, but rather because I just didn't want to interact with him at all. He didn't have the same problem, usually having some demeaning look, or making some belittling utterance whenever I came into the room.

Many were the times that he'd give me a dressing down over my shortcomings, as he saw them, uttering what became a favorite slogan, "You're never going to amount to a tinker's damn." I never have learned what a *tinker's damn* is, but I sometimes suspect that he thought that if he prophesied that enough, it would eventually come true.

It had just the opposite effect.

Due, no doubt, to my very low self-esteem, but also because I was determined to deprive him of the satisfaction of being right in that respect, I worked earnestly to be the best I could be at whatever job I was doing.

Having started school too early, at just four years old, I was always "the dumb kid." That came to an end in my junior year of high school, when I suddenly discovered that I was just as capable of getting good grades as anyone else.

At eighteen, after graduating from high school, I enlisted in the U.S. Air Force, being trained in the maintenance of electronic navigation equipment on "SAC" B-52 bombers and KC-135 refueling aircraft. The *Strategic Air Command* was the Air Force's premier echelon during those Cold War years. Within my four-year enlistment I became an expert in my field; the one they called whenever there was a dire emergency or a tough problem to solve. Even as a lower-ranking airman, I became a shift supervisor, was eventually named Outstanding Airman of the 4228th Strategic Wing, and then again of the 4th Air Division, and was then promoted to "buck sergeant" well ahead of anyone else at my level, even second term airmen with much more time in grade.

After being honorably discharged from the Air Force, I went to work for a company from London, England that manufactured electronic color sorting machines; machines with "eyes"—photosensitive scanners, that were used to process commodities like beans, peanuts, walnuts, and food products like diced carrots and dehydrated potatoes, and even pebbles dredged up in the harbor at San Diego, the machines separating the good from the bad to improve the grade of the product and thereby enhance its selling price. I traveled all over the country, from east coast to west, and from north to south.

Then it was a local engineering company that manufactured rotary electronic components which were used mostly in military/aerospace instruments like gyroscopes, some used by NASA's Gemini Project.

And finally it was a company in Holland, Michigan that designed and manufactured specialized test chambers for the military/aerospace industry, where I eventually taught myself how to design and develop electronic controls using cutting edge linear monolithic integrated circuits, and became a division manager with a seat on the company's Executive Committee.

All this left my dad scratching his head. If he ever had second thoughts about me, he never mentioned them, but he eventually did quit with the disparaging remarks.

I can take credit for some of this success, and of course I have to credit my dad's negative attitude towards me as something that always motivated me to prove him wrong.

But as I reflect back on all the jobs I had, beginning as a twelve-year old boy, a common thread or, more accurately, an *uncommon* thread, runs through them all. I excelled in every job I ever had, because in each and every case, I genuinely liked and respected the person I was working for, and that person genuinely liked and respected me. I never saw any of my employers or supervisors as *the boss*, but always instead as a friend, and usually a mentor. These relationships always brought me advantages and opportunities above and beyond what might have been ordinary and appropriate for someone in my position. Because I was liked and appreciated, these people wanted to do good things for me.

This didn't happen because I was smart, or as a strategy that I'd learned somewhere along the way. It just happened to always work out that way. Perhaps I was subconsciously avoiding people I didn't like so didn't apply for jobs where such people would be in charge, and it's just common sense that those I did happen to click with would also have had similar feelings for me. But one doesn't usually get to choose his boss, at least not in the beginning when working in entry level jobs, and certainly never as an enlisted man in the military.

I never realized it at the time, tending always to take credit for everything and brag about how I was a "self made man." But I am finally convinced that all this was really the result of something much different—that I was actually being placed into these situations by a silent and invisible benefactor; my old friend "Bill."

6
A Moment of Clarity

After eight years at the company in Holland, I was thirty-five years old, had accomplished everything I'd ever dreamed of achieving. I lived in a cozy ground floor apartment, had a really flashy car, money in the bank, went to work every day neatly dressed in slacks, a white shirt and tie, and on my own schedule. I was in great physical condition, *tall, dark and handsome* as it were, and (although I wasn't aware of it because of my perverse self image) sexually attractive to young women. I was the picture of success and the envy of many guys my age.

And I was not happy.

In fact, I was beginning to feel more like a loser than ever before. Perhaps part of it was because my dad had died about a year before, so I no longer had anyone to blame, or prove myself to. But because of my avoidant personality, I also had no close relationships, and felt utterly alone, even when the center of attention and surrounded by colleagues at the company.

I began spending a lot of time at the Lake Michigan beach during the warm months, often observing the families who came out to the lake in the early evening hours, and being especially affected by scenes of fathers playing with their young sons. At my age, I was sure that would never be me; that I had missed the opportunity to marry young and raise a family of my own; that there was nothing left for me but divorcees or widows with some other guy's children, which was a prospect I didn't care to contemplate.

As my career in Holland became progressively less and less rewarding, I became increasingly restless and disinterested. I finally decided to try starting a business of my own, and resigned.

That soon seemed like a big mistake.

When I left the company, it was only with the vague notion that I'd keep doing what I'd been doing there; designing and manufacturing electronic controls. I took the next two or three months off, doing nothing but trying to enjoy my freedom from responsibilities as my bank balance began to decline. When I finally began to get serious about my entrepreneurial project, the realities began to become glaringly visible.

While I understood that success would be all about marketing and sales, I was an engineer, had always thought like and engineer, and had no marketing and sales skills at all. I had made a name for myself in the industry, the company's competitors knowing that we'd gained an edge on them because of the instruments and controls that I'd been developing. It looked like my best bet at that point was to take advantage of that personal asset, by developing, manufacturing and selling the same sorts of products to these competitors. But I couldn't bring myself to do that to my previous employer, a good man who had given so much to me, generally making me what I was, and who was still a close friend. It just seemed too much like betrayal.

So I began to look for other opportunities. As time went on, I continued to live the lifestyle that I'd become accustomed to over the past few years, spending freely, even though my income was zero. And the balance in my bank account continued to diminish.

These were realities that I hadn't really given much thought to before making what had really been an emotional decision; to give up my job and leave the company in Holland. They weren't the only realities; there was something much more devastating!

It had never occurred to me that outside of my acquaintances at work, I had no friends. I didn't even know any of the neighbors in my own apartment building. Outside of business trips, seminars, and local company functions, I also had no social life; no interaction with other people at all, except for the time spent in certain local restaurants, where I was "a regular."

I had never ordered take out or prepared meals at home. In fact, having previously been in the habit of taking work home and laboring over it into the wee hours on my dining nook table, I'd always used my refrigerator as a storage cabinet for drafting tools and office supplies. As my already seriously depleted bank account continued to shrink, I became sensitive to the cost of eating every meal out and gradually began to change that expensive habit, skipping meals when I wasn't actually hungry, and making do, at least part of the time, with fast food. Unfortunately, I found that there is no social interaction at places like McDonald's and Burger King. These places had no real group of regulars; I was just another number on a receipt, waiting for my order to come up.

The only good thing about these places was the children. Because they offered inexpensive kid's meals, they were popular with upwardly mobile families on a tight schedule during the dinner hour, and it was somehow uplifting to observe the kids; always so animated and worry free. Outside of that ... not so much. Earlier in the day, except for the lunch hour rush, these places catered to seniors and took on the atmosphere of a retirement home. In the evenings, after the dinner hour, they became hangouts for behaviorally challenged teenagers and, to a lesser extent, adults who usually appeared to be stuck at or below the poverty level.

Feeling conspicuously out of place amongst fast food clientele, I finally bought myself a pair of blue jeans. I'd never owned a pair of blue jeans in my entire life!

I didn't feel like a young, successful executive anymore. I wasn't part of the family scene, and I didn't fit in with the evening crowd either, even with the blue jeans. In fact, I didn't fit in anywhere. I began to feel utterly alone in life, and less and less interested in going out. Instead, I spent a lot of time napping, and becoming increasingly depressed.

The loneliness steadily grew until it actually became physically painful and the depression became frighteningly debilitating. I'd finally reached the end of my rope; what some have called the *moment of clarity*. I felt totally isolated from the normal, everyday rest of the world, was utterly hopeless, and had no idea what to do about it. I didn't want to live like this anymore. But I was perfectly healthy! Surely I wasn't going to die of natural causes any time soon, no matter how fervently I wished for that solution.

And I knew that suicide wouldn't work for me.

I'd tried that too many times before when I was a teenager, and had always chickened out at the last minute.

As a boy, my first attempt was a hangman's noose, made like those in the old movie westerns and fastened to the rafters in our basement. Standing on a stool, I'd placed it around my neck, and all I had to do was fall off the stool—or even one quick slip and I would have been a goner. But it never happened. I'd always wind up the same way; crying in frustration over not having the courage to go through with it.

As a young teenager I developed an interest in electronics. I'd get old radios from my uncle's junk yard, the kind that were big pieces of furniture with huge old fashioned electron tubes with two-digit nomenclatures—"15," "86," "45," and so on—which used high voltage DC power supplies. As an alternative to hanging myself, I thought that electrocution might be better, since once it began to fry my brain, I would not be able to stop it. So I wired the high voltage to electrodes connected with white bandaging tape between eyelids and my temples, and began to turn up the power. All I remember about that is visions of spiraling rings developing in my brain as the current increased. I can't remember ever pulling the plug, so don't know what stopped it. Perhaps I just passed out and the wires became disconnected because of perspiration.

At some point later on, a plastic bag seemed like a good solution. I'd pull a plastic bag over my head and tape it around my neck, with the idea that the air in it would slowly become depleted of oxygen; I'd peacefully pass out, and would surely then be unable to prevent myself from being asphyxiated. That probably would have worked, except that as the oxygen in the bag became depleted and replaced by carbon dioxide, my breathing rate steadily increased until I was fiercely panting. With the inside surfaces of the bag becoming covered with condensation, I was no longer able to see the outside world. My head and face were burning up, and I was sweating profusely. But I never lost consciousness. As many times as I tried to end my life this way, just before blacking out, something would always make me rip the bag open, admitting fresh air, which always felt clean and cool and nice.

As I think back on all these sorry episodes in my young life, it occurs to me that although as a young teenage boy I owned not only my own 12-guage shotgun, but also a Winchester 32-Special rifle, I can't remember ever thinking about using either one of these weapons on myself. That seems strange indeed, since both of these were kept in my bedroom closet, and were therefore readily available. One would think that shooting myself would have been the first thought that occurred to me. Perhaps I thought it would have been too messy, or not sufficiently dramatic.

I finally came to realize that nobody feels sorry for suicides; that except for instances prompted by medical conditions—a brain tumor or the untreatable and unbearable pain of some terminal condition—most people are apt to see suicide as the fool's way out, and a disgrace for the remaining family to forever bear.

After all my boyish experiments with suicide as the only way to end all the fear and unhappiness in our home, for me at least, it seems remarkable that I'm still around to write about them. Nobody else ever knew about any of these many attempts, so it wasn't about feigning suicide as a way to get someone's attention or sympathy. It was about feeling like I was caught up in a situation that I had no power to do anything about. Death ultimately seemed like the only way out. But each time it approached, something inside me would, at the last minute, spark a glimmer of hope, just enough to convey the message that life wouldn't be like this forever.

I usually attributed my failures to my lack of courage, and I'd curse myself for it. But I think it's more likely that it was the proverbial *still, small voice...*

Bill's still, small voice.

―――

Be all that as it may, here I was, decades later, in the same predicament, but without the suicide option. Thus it seemed like the only hope left for me was to die of some natural cause, or somehow change; the *moment of clarity* was at hand—*change or die.*

But with a third of my life already gone—the best years, I supposed at that point—I was solidly set in my ways. I had no idea how to change, and I knew that I was not capable of changing anything on my own. I felt like I had, for some unknown and unfair reason, been singled out for this abuse. I couldn't understand, *why me?* I was not a bad person; no worse, at least, than many others. In fact, I'd known lots of people who were much less likable than me, who still had a life. Why didn't I get to be just like everybody else; happily married, with a home and family of my own; with someone who cared about me?

I was not religious. I'd grown up in the protestant tradition as a good Presbyterian boy, but that ended in my early teenage years. During my time in the Air Force, a group of us airmen sometimes went to church, but that was mostly just a Sunday morning something-to-do that began with cinnamon toast and coffee at the Holiday Inn, followed by a late arrival at some church or another, alternating between the denominations represented within our group of six to eight guys. We were never really serious worshipers. I hadn't been in a church since. I had actually become impatient with religious people, church-going or not, and avoided them as much as possible.

But I'd finally hit bottom, and found myself falling on my knees beside my dining room table tearfully pleading, *"God, I don't know how to change this. If you can't change it, please let me die!"*

7
A Complex Miracle

Dining on Sunday nights in Grand Haven was always a problem back then, the town still being somewhat provincial in the mid-1970s. Most of the restaurants were closed, else closed early. In better times that didn't make any difference, because I seldom patronized any restaurants in Grand Haven anyway. More often I'd choose the *Horizon Room* at the Muskegon County Airport, or the Holiday Inn in Spring Lake.

On the Sunday night following the *moment of clarity* incident, feeling that I couldn't stand being alone, I drove up to Muskegon hoping to spend some time with the Horizon Room's regulars or possibly with one of the Drelles brothers—Gus, Pete or Leo, the Greeks who ran the place. That turned out to be just the right thing. During dinner I had a very engaging conversation with Peter Drelles, and after that spent and hour or more drinking coffee and smoking cigarettes in the company of several other regular customers, mostly airport concession and staff people.

The experience was great, and I left the airport feeling happy and almost normal for the first time in several weeks.

That didn't last long.

It was ten miles from my apartment complex to "MKG"—the Muskegon County Airport. About half way back home, traveling south along US-31 towards Grand Haven in the dark of a moonless night, my car suddenly died. This was not good. The weather had suddenly turned cold, and the chill wind blowing across the still-warm waters of Lake Michigan was bringing in snow flurries. Not usually having any need to anticipate such situations, I wasn't dressed for the occasion. There were of course, no cell phones in the mid-1970s, and the traffic along US-31 on Sunday nights was sparse.

It wasn't just that the engine had stalled or run out of gas or anything like that. The car was completely dead, not even any dome or dash lights. Luckily I'd been able to coast far enough to get it off the highway and onto the grassy shoulder of the road. Also luckily, a rather scruffy guy in a beat-up old pickup truck saw me standing there outside my car in my shirtsleeves scratching my head, and stopped to see what was going on. He was headed south through Grand Haven, so willingly offered to take me into town.

One of my apartment building neighbors was Gil Johnson, an older guy who operated a Standard Oil service station downtown. In spite of the late hour, I knocked at his door and explained my predicament. Without hesitation, Gil fetched his jacket, took me downtown with him to get his tow truck, and together we went out to haul my car in to his station. The next day he and Rodney, his young blonde, wavy-haired assistant, tore into it in search of the problem, expecting to find a dead short somewhere in the car's wiring harness.

That evening, Gil had a mild heart attack.

That left Rod all alone at the station, pumping gas, changing oil, fixing tires, and doing all the other routine service station jobs, and with very little time left over to work on my dismantled Oldsmobile. He really didn't have the knowledge and skills needed to find the problems and put the car back together anyway. So I was just plainly out of luck for the indefinite future as far as wheels were concerned. In better times I wouldn't have needed to care; I would have just rented a car to use until mine was back on the road. But now it was plain that I was going to be a pedestrian for a little while.

During the week that wasn't much of a problem, because the bank had a branch right across the street from the apartment complex I called home. It was located on the corner of a small commercial area that also included a W.T. Grants department store, a small supermarket, and a couple of restaurants. So I could get money and whatever else I needed by simply walking across the boulevard.

But Sunday nights were another matter. There was only one restaurant in town that was open on Sunday nights, and that was a dingy, smoke-filled 24-hour place a little over a mile away on the north side, called the *Rendezvous*.

I'd been there only once before, back when it was just a little hamburger stand with a few homemade plywood booths, and owned by a gruff old man who worked alone, cooking the hamburgers and pushing them through a little service window for people to fetch and bring to their table themselves. It had since been much expanded, and now had cooks and waitresses, but since having become a 24-hour place, it had also gained the unseemly distinction as being a hangout for losers with dubious reputations.

Everything about the restaurant's two or three expansion projects had been cheaply and amateurishly done, one result of which was the wholly inadequate ventilation system. The place always smelled like dirty carpeting or, perhaps, like its clientele were typically people who were seriously in need of a bath. The cigarette smoke was so dense most of the time that it made one's eyes burn and itch, and everything was covered with its residue. After sitting in the Rendezvous for an hour, everyone left smelling like an ashtray, regardless of whether they were smokers, or not. It was rumored that after dark a healthy drug trade was carried on in the restaurant's parking lot, and around 2:30 am, as all the taverns and bars closed for the night, many of their patrons would move on to the Rendezvous. And what a strange, uncouth and unsightly bunch they were—men who felt free to sexually harass the waitresses, while burping, belching and farting at will; a gaggle of weird looking characters such as were never seen on the streets of Grand Haven during daylight hours. As might be expected, the police were also occasional visitors to the Rendezvous in the wee hours, being called to break up fights and eject drunken, obnoxious and trouble-making customers.

I'd never really fancied myself as better than anyone else, and as a result of my dwindling financial reserves, I'd already gotten used to dining in places without tablecloths. But the Rendezvous, nevertheless, was definitely not my kind of place. Suspecting that might be obvious to the late-night crowd, and fearing that what they'd perceive as an uppity demeanor might give rise to altercations, after a couple of late-night visits, I never went back to the place again at that time of day. And even at any other time of day, I felt uneasy about the possibility of being seen there by anyone I knew. There was, of course, never really much chance of that ever happening.

At the Rendezvous, I mostly kept to myself. I didn't care to become a regular there, not even a Sunday night regular. But after a while I got into the habit of going there for lunch. I found that the lunch hour crowd was different, consisting mostly of working people who didn't have time to sit around and smoke, and with daylight streaming in through the windows to brighten the place, it didn't look as dingy as it always did at night. Besides that, they served real food there, and at cheap prices—lunch specials like spaghetti, Hungarian goulash, roast beef with boiled potatoes and carrots—choices much more appetizing and healthful than hamburgers and French fries.

The days went by, Gil was still convalescing, my car was still in pieces inside his service station, and I was still walking. Sometimes at night, if she wasn't doing anything else, my widowed mother would pick me up, and we'd go to the Rendezvous together. One Sunday night she pointed out one of the waitresses and asked, "Who is that girl?"

"What girl?" I replied.

"That girl over there. The one with the long dark hair."

"I don't know. She's never waited on me. I think her name is Patty. Why?"

She just shrugged and shook her head, as if to indicate 'Oh, no reason. I just wondered.' and the conversation turned to something else.

The following afternoon, as I was leaving the restaurant after what was either a very late lunch, or a very early dinner, "that girl" took me by the arm, pulling me aside into an unoccupied dining area called "the green room"—a not very imaginative name derived from the fact that the carpeting and upholstery in that room were shades of dark green. She somewhat embarrassedly handed me a smoke-blue envelope containing a greeting card.

I guessed that there had been some mistake; was it an invitation—or had she somehow gotten the impression that it was my birthday? After reading the card, it was then my turn to be uncomfortable and embarrassed. I've forgotten exactly how the card expressed it, but the gist of the message was 'Can we be friends?'

I was thirty-five years old going on thirty-six. She was young, pretty, attractively slim, and neatly groomed, and should have been my "dream come true." For whatever reason, she had apparently fallen for me—as my mother had so easily noticed the night before. Since whatever she'd noticed had been going right over the top of my oblivious head, in desperation, this poor girl had resorted to the greeting card.

But Patty was also only eighteen years old. Getting up my best avoidant demeanor, I gently explained that I was sincerely flattered, but wasn't that kind of guy; the kind who would take advantage of a teenager's crush. Attempting to let her down gently, I suggested that she could, and someday probably would, do better with someone closer to her own age.

On the way back to my apartment that late afternoon, I hated myself for being so dumb; for never having noticed that this girl was so keenly interested in me, and for so stupidly dismissing that chance for a relationship.

———

Somewhere during all this time, Gil Johnson had gotten back on his feet and went back to work downtown. He and Rod put my car back together, and I was mobile again. As it turned out, there really wasn't anything more seriously wrong than a bad alternator and a dead battery, something that could have been easily diagnosed and promptly fixed without having to tear the whole car apart. How could Gil, a long-experienced auto mechanic, have gotten so confused!

But by that time I'd become more comfortable about patronizing the Rendezvous. After the card incident with Patty, I began to make late lunches a habit; lunches as late as 2:30 in the afternoon so I'd be there when her shift started at three o'clock. Soon I was going there for dinner just before her break time, finding a table in the back dining room near what the staff used as their break table, and it wasn't long before she and I would be spending her break time together. Not long after that, I began to show up at eleven o'clock at night, around the time when she got off work, and we'd sit for a while talking and drinking coffee together.

As our relationship grew, parting became more and more difficult and the after-work conversations moved to my apartment, with me ultimately driving her home at four or five in the morning and wondering why her father was never there waiting with a shotgun.

My ambivalence about our difference in age continued as annoying background noise. As we became ever closer, the prospect of reality setting in and ending this wonderful episode was always in the back of my mind. Even had I been able to dismiss it, there were several well meaning people around, mainly female family members, who'd gently suggest that someone was going to get hurt before this affair was all over. Those on Patty's side were expressing similar concerns, wondering what she could possibly see in a man so much older; her mother disgustedly suggesting that she'd too soon wind up pushing me around in a wheelchair.

At one point, having become painfully convinced that they were all probably right, I decided to call it off. She was hurt, but would have none of it; suggesting that perhaps the immaturity was on *my* side, and maybe it was time for *me* to think about growing up!

The next afternoon, as we lay together atop the bed in my apartment just before it was time for her to go to work, I had what, for lack of any better description, was a *vision*. As I lay there staring at the shotcrete ceiling, fretting about the previous night's episode, and worrying about our prospects for the future, or lack thereof, the ceiling seemed to open up, and a kindly face smiled down on the two of us. The message was clear. We were destined to be together. There was no longer any reason to have doubts.

I asked for her hand on Valentine's Day, and we were married the first weekend of the following July.

The days between February 14th and July 9th of 1977 were the happiest of my life. We were as carefree as children, all was right with the world, and everything was fun. Life in love was so good, in fact, that it would have been worth all of those thirty-six more difficult years just to be able to experience these 21-weeks of wonder and joy.

There was never a groom who stood at the front of a church with greater pride as he watched his bride come down the center isle on her father's arm. The older women in my family, especially my mother and my favorite aunt, Aunt Aggie, were overjoyed that at long last I'd finally found a wife. I'm sure most of the guys were thinking, 'You lucky sonofagun!' as Patty came down the isle, more beautiful than I'd ever seen her before ... more beautiful than even I would have imagined she ever could be!

And there was a reason for that exceptional beauty. We didn't know it at the time, but she was three or four weeks pregnant. The second part of the dream was already becoming true!

As I write this over 36-years later, she is still here, and during our time together we have experienced all the things those traditional wedding vows foresee; for better and for worse, for richer and for poorer, in good times and in bad, in sickness and in health, in joys and in sorrows. And all in the company of five wonderful children.

How did this all come about?

(1) On that night so long ago, there I was, unemployed, broke, and alone. I seemed to be different than everybody else. I didn't know why. Was I any worse than anyone else? Was there some reason why I was so much less deserving of happiness? The answer to all those questions was "No," leaving me with the feeling that some invisible forces were conspiring against me. All my previous efforts to be somebody and to be loved by somebody had failed. I was nobody, and there was nobody who cared about me. After a-quarter of a century of struggling to make a life for myself, I'd totally failed. It was plain to see: for whatever reasons, I was incapable of being anything different than what I was, a loner and a loser. I was tired of trying. I gave up, throwing my future to the fates. If this was destined to forever be my lot in life, I didn't want to live any longer. I went to bed, hoping as I fell asleep that I'd never wake up.

(2) My car was still fairly new; a slick Oldsmobile Cutlass-S 2-door, carnival red on the outside tastefully accented with white pin stripes, with a white vinyl top and a comfortable white leather interior. It was a fine, flashy car, and I'd always taken very good care of it. It suddenly and inexplicably died.

(3) Gil Johnson, my neighbor, had been in the business so long that his gas station in downtown Grand Haven was almost an institution as he neared retirement. He was a good mechanic with a lifetime of experience. For

reasons unknown, when it came to diagnosing the problem with my car, he was totally fooled, assuming that it was something much more difficult than it actually was, and tearing the car apart in search of it.

(4) Then Gil had a mild myocardial infarction, taking him out of the picture for a while.

(5) Being temporarily without wheels, I was forced to capitulate, swallow my pride, and patronize the Rendezvous, a place I'd always shunned before, but the only restaurant within walking distance on Sunday nights.

(6) In spite of the Rendezvous' dubious reputation and rough edges, a very decent young girl had just recently found a job there; a girl from an upper-middle class family living in a classy subdivision on Spring Lake called Harbor Point: Patricia Marie Cappel, a girl who for whatever reasons, and with no encouragement on my part, found herself strongly attracted to me.

(7) During the ensuing romance, my lingering ambivalence was finally dispelled once and for all by an apparition; the face in the ceiling of my bedroom.

(8) We were married, had children, and have been living happily and successfully together ever after.

My original situation could readily be diagnosed as the inevitable outcome for a young man with a strongly entrenched avoidant personality adjustment, and all the rest could be attributed to a very strange, but fortunate, set of coincidences—until the *face in the ceiling* incident.

As is usually the case with such experiences, that just happened without any inducement or provocation, not a response to meditation, prayer, or any other sort of petition or invitation, nor the result of a blow to the head, drugs or drunkenness. As is also usually the case, if asked to give a detailed description of the face, or the experience, I wouldn't be able to say more than what has already been said: "a kindly face smiled down, somehow communicating the message that we were supposed to be together, that there were no reasons for concern."

I eventually came to understand that it was Bill again! Had he any shoulders to shrug and a head to wag he probably would have been doing that as he reluctantly acknowledged that I'd become a hopeless case, and decided that it was time to enter the picture again to save the day and get me back on track.

And it wouldn't be the last time.

8
The Second Apparition

The euphoria of the love affair gradually faded in the face of life's realities. The lovers turned into partners as the family grew, and as our business found a niche and began to prosper. I was well into living the dreams that I'd had so long ago while sitting atop my car in the evenings at the Lake Michigan beach, watching families play together.

For most of my life, I had remained a loner—not by choice, but simply because as a child I'd perfected the art of avoiding close relationships. That was now in the past, yet there remained a part of me that was still a loner of sorts, a part that needed a certain amount of solitude. I often had that time at night, after my family had gone off to their beds; in the wee hours after they had all fallen asleep. In the peace and quiet of those hours, I could efficiently take care of the day's business paperwork, catch up on correspondence, work on new product designs, study, or read.

One such night, after nine wonderfully halcyonic years, while sitting at the computer in our family room where I usually burned the midnight oil, I suddenly sensed that I was not alone—that there was a presence, as if someone looking over my left shoulder. Assuming it was my wife or one of the kids, perhaps having trouble sleeping and gotten up for a drink of water or a snack, I was not disturbed and continued with my attention focused on what I was doing. After several minutes with them just standing quietly there at my shoulder, I turned in my chair to see ... *nothing*. There was no one there. Yet, when I turned back to my work, I still had the same feeling that someone was standing just behind me, looking over my left shoulder. From that moment on, wherever I went within the house that evening and whatever I did, I could not shake the feeling that someone was following.

The next morning I woke up with the unsettling feeling that it was not just a figment of my imagination, nor a hallucination caused by fatigue at that late hour the night before. I also soon realized it was still there. Not long after I had gotten up, the sensation reappeared, as if someone tagging along behind or beside me.

At that point, this became frightening. Was I having a nervous breakdown, or losing my mind altogether? Was I dying; was this the angel who would take me, or maybe the devil coming to claim his due.

Yet, it did not really feel like that sort of situation. In fact, this presence felt friendly, even comforting in a way. I began getting used to it during the next couple of days, and liked having it around. While doing my best to act perfectly normal, and not mentioning any of this to anyone, in my thoughts I talked to it, and eventually it began to talk back.

It was a boy; a nice boy, without an age, of course, but feeling like about ten or twelve. He became my constant companion, getting up with me in the morning, sharing in everything I did throughout the day, and crawling back into bed and snuggling up beside me at night. He was beautiful. He was loving. He was awesome in every way. I was in love all over again.

What would others think were they to become aware of what was going on in my head? Was I becoming schizoid? What else could this be? Although actually an apparition, this boy was entirely real to me and I loved him dearly. In these few days, I had become as happy as I had ever been since the days of unexpectedly falling in love and marrying my remarkable young wife. My heart was full of joy, and I felt a wonderful peace and contentment.

Then, about two weeks after the boy first came to me, he said, "I have to go now." A prolonged silent dialog followed. I did not want him to leave and begged him to stay with me. For two days I agonized over the realization that this obviously could not go on, that it wasn't real, that maybe I *was* loosing my mind. But I still did not want him to go. And he kept trying to make me understand that he could not stay.

On the morning of the third day, he hugged me, clinging to me tightly and whispering, "I have to go now, but I'll always be with you."

As I felt his presence begin to fade, the tears began streaming down my cheeks, and I hurried away to a private place where nobody would see me crying over something I would not be able to talk about.

How could I explain this to anyone? Surely they would think I was in the grips of an emotional crisis, and badly in need of help!

On finally sharing my story confidentially with a very sensitive and intuitive friend, he was immediately able to interpret what had happened. The boy was me; the *me* that had gone into hiding so many years ago, and had finally found the courage to come back out. He had come to show me the boy I had really been, a boy who was beautiful, loving and awesome in every way, a boy who bore no resemblance whatsoever to the image of myself that I had carried around in my mind for forty-six years, an image that had spoiled what could have been some of the best years of my life.

I immediately realized that my friend was right, and then I understood what "I have to go now, but I'll always be with you." meant.

It was true that since falling in love, marrying and having children, I had pretty much gotten over my avoidant personality. But it was also true that I had never dealt with what caused it in the first place. Children in problem families almost always grow up with a sense of guilt, vaguely believing that they're as much at fault as any others in the family. That's a real shame! A child cannot choose the family that they're born into, and if, by the luck of the draw, that happens to be a dysfunctional family, it doesn't have to be defining of that child. Yet all too often that's exactly what happens.

This strange episode was, without a doubt, instigated by Bill. I had indeed gotten over my AvPD, but that hadn't done much to boost my self-esteem. As a result, not only did I harbor secret doubts about ever being able to succeed in what had become our family business, I was also unconsciously sending the wrong sorts of signals to our children, signals suggesting that we were, for reasons beyond our understanding and control, destined to be less deserving of success and respect than others, and that they should adjust their aspirations accordingly. For the sake of the business, and for the good of our children, that needed to change, and Bill evidently took it upon himself to see to it that it did.

Although I know that many intelligent and well-meaning people might dismiss this as the delusions of a crackpot, I have no doubts about it. As Carl Jung once said:

"... such experiences bring with them absolute certainty, as anyone who has ever been seized with one knows. It is a certainty that comes from within. It cannot be analyzed because the experience is overwhelmingly supernatural, with the mind operating in realms man knows nothing about as yet, and possibly never will."

As I write about this these many years later, looking back upon it as impartially as all this intervening time now permits, I am even more overwhelmed with amazement and wonder! Once again, this episode was something that just came *out of the blue*, as it were, not as an answer to prayer or the result of any other sort of meditation or conscious preoccupation with personal issues. Unlike the "face in the ceiling" incident, this one was not just a flash in the pan, but was instead something that went on for several days and nights, something that could hardly be dismissed as a momentary disturbance in the brain. And, thinking about the essence of it, how else could I ever have gotten to know the boy who had been me as he really was, except to have had this experience?

There were several adults in my young life, who obviously thought a great deal of me. These and others might have tried to convince me that I had actually been a very nice boy; a very decent boy. But I could easily dismiss their very positive opinions, and even their affection, by asserting in my most avoidant manner that they didn't really know me. Only by actually spending time together as the most intimate of friends with the boy I actually was, could I ever have come to believe the truth, and that's what Bill had somehow arranged.

Whatever you choose to believe, the fact is that this was indeed a life changing experience for me and my family.

If not Bill, then who or what?

9
A Final Appearance

Several months after the boy episode, I experienced another strange and unsettling presence, this one gender neutral and very brief, but no less profound and meaningful.

Alone again, this time in my office in the late afternoon hours, I was engrossed in catching up on some long neglected paperwork when the ambiance suddenly and dramatically changed. All of the familiar sights, sounds and surroundings dissolved from my awareness, as if I had been transported to another place where there was nothingness, just me and a conspicuous, but invisible, *presence.*

I actually saw nothing with my eyes, yet in my memory there is an image of a figure that was tall, featureless, and blue; dark blue and indistinct, as if perhaps draped from head to toe in a full length shroud, and chimerically wavering, like a reflection on water or a form seen through heat waves in the air.

Nothing was said, but somehow I was struck with the realization that I was in the presence of something much superior to me, and as my mind was transported to the place where this *something* had come from, I experienced a realm more perfectly pure and without fault or flaw than the human mind is capable of fathoming. As often as I have tried to describe this apparition, words have failed. None of the superlatives in the English language seem adequate; all of them seem to apply, yet even in combination they fall far short of the sublimity of whatever this was.

I felt so small and ashamed, and utterly unfit to be in the presence of such a figure, yet overjoyed by having, for who knows what reason, been found worthy of such a palatine revelation.

A new general view of our terrible world suddenly took form in my mind. All my life I have known the myth about Adam and Eve's Garden of Eden. I understood that we humans had become stubbornly self-centered and dark spirited, even sometimes downright evil; that we had fallen far from what we originally were. But until that evening, I had never really realized *how far* we had fallen, or how awful we had made our world.

We are born into the mess our ancestors have created. It is all we know. We become accustomed to living with dark things, our *seven deadly sins*, which lead to hate, shame, and guilt. Success in life is, for us, merely to avoid wretchedness or an untimely death.

The utter perfection that stood before me showed with profound clarity the depths to which we have fallen. So far separated are we from that kind of perfection and purity that our situation seemed tragically hopeless. The chasm was so wide; how could man ever rise back up to approach anything worthy of deliverance?

We abide indeed, like a man fallen into a cesspool who, frightened and struggling, is barely able to keep his head above the stinking muck. He lives, but helplessly, at the bottom of that pit, ever hopeful that someday, somehow, someone will come along and raise him up. And such are we, ever copiously replenishing the contents of the cesspool we are drowning in.

And yet, in spite of it all, the *cosmics* evidently remain faithful to us. Else, what was this *something* standing here in my office, having come to show me the difference between what we are, and what we once were and could again be?

And I wondered, why me? Who am I that such perfection would concern itself with me? I am nothing. I am worse than nothing, since I am equal among all those who err and hate, and suffer the consequential shame and guilt.

I sat there in my office armchair and stupidly wept; utterly ashamed and broken hearted.

As this fantasy faded back into reality, this *something*, this indigo ghost, left with a message: "Well done." I did not understand what that meant. What had been *well done?* I had no idea then, nor did I have for a long time after.

I do now.

In spite of all the experiences I've described in the foregoing pages, I still had doubts about my *Bill*. As time went on and the immediacy of these experiences faded, so did their believability. It was always easier to believe that all these things were merely figments of my superstitious mind and/or my overactive imagination. Much of that is the result of *peer pressure*; conformity always being strongly impelled by the need to be accepted by others; to not be considered different and become an oddity or social outcast.

I now understand that the "indigo ghost" was just Bill again, whose purpose was to remove all doubt once and for all, and to instill in me the more sensible ethic of living one day at a time.

After this episode, I never again wavered in my belief that Bill, my cosmic companion, was real, and I had no choice but to believe that he dwelt in another realm, a place of primordial consciousness and perfection surpassing all human understanding. But there was another equally important truth that Bill intended to impart.

In our culture we are taught the ethic of delayed gratification; to slog through each day diligently and courageously in anticipation of future rewards. I was no exception. I was working long hours, and usually seven days a week, at building the business and what I thought would someday be a comfortable and secure future for my wife and children. That seemed like the right thing to do, but in fact it was depriving our children of the love and nurturing that a more attentive father would happily lavish upon them.

In my brief vision, I saw the gaping disparity between what was probably the place we envisage as *heaven* and our life here on earth, and sadly I then understood that there are none in this earthly realm who would come anywhere close to deserving an eternity in that one, no matter how diligently and courageously, or righteously, we tried to pursue that end.

The lesson imparted was clear; this is the *only* life most of us will ever have. It comes as a gift, not with burdens of responsibility. On finding ourselves alive in this world, our place is merely to accept the gift of life with gratitude, to discover its wonders, and to delight in the opportunities that each day brings, without worrying about what has been, or what might be. We are not partners in creation, but rather transient beneficiaries of it. We are *mortal*; a short time here and then forever gone. How wasteful of our one life is our obsession with success, as measured by superficialities—by attractiveness, affluence and achievement!

Happiness and security are the true measures of success in life. That accrues only within our relationships with each other. From that point forward, I began to invest in our family first, rather than in the business, understanding that our individual personal assets are infinitely more important and enduring than those which can be enumerated on a balance sheet.

Now that our children are mostly all grown up, all different, but all in their own way happy and successful, and some with children of their own, *that* has proven to have been the right thing to do.

※

10
Forsaken

I would hear directly from Bill only two more times.

The first was a very brief visit to let me know that I was *forsaken*. That did not come as a surprise, since I'd realized that ever since his revelations as the visiting "indigo ghost." I was not sure what his purpose was in making that clear.

It might have been because in relating that episode to others, most refused to accept the proposition that we mortals, living in this realm, fall so far short of what I experienced in that vision, that it was unlikely that any of our souls would ever be welcomed to that other place. Almost everyone I know has grown up in the Christian tradition, and has been taught the "good news;" that there is a paradisiacal afterlife for the truly faithful. My *bad news* was therefore never well received, and was usually dismissed out of hand. In the face of all that rejection, I tended to question that proposition myself.

But then came Bill again, confirming what I already knew to be true. Once again, the message was not that I was such a low and unworthy person that the gift of an edenic eternity was out of the question for the likes of me, but rather that I was living the gift right now; that I, and everyone else, should seek joy in this life; the only life we'll have.

We are indeed not "partners in creation," as we are often taught by those who are obsessed with a need to believe that we are each special, and born for a particular purpose. But rather than being satisfied with the world we are born into, we have become its despoilers. Life in this realm is often trying and unpleasant, and that is not because creation is imperfect or incomplete. The reasons for that have been known since the most ancient times: *pride, covetousness, lust, envy, gluttony, anger,* and *sloth*.

These are the *capital vices*, also known as the "seven deadly sins." Although in our culture this is usually considered to be a Christian construct, all religions and philosophies across the world and in all times have had a similar code.

Bill's message was clear; that before this life is over, before the gift is gone, I could live it more joyously and abundantly by seeing these flaws in myself, and getting over these destructive habits.

A simple matter indeed but, after a lifetime of conditioning by the culture that we're born into, not an easy thing to do. Nevertheless, benefits would certainly accrue from at least trying.

Most religions have some concept of a life after death. There is evidence that even the earliest of humans, the Neanderthals, laid their dead to rest with this in mind. It seems perfectly understandable that this would be so, since human beings over all these tens of thousands of years would have, without doubt, had encounters with cosmics, and it is very comforting to believe that there is a connection, or a portal of some sort, between this world and theirs.

Christians have a concept of heaven, a paradise awaiting them, but have some trouble deciding for sure exactly what it takes to get there; whether it's about *works* or *grace*. The bad news, and the good news, is that it's a moot question, since there is, in fact, no afterlife for us. Cosmics are cosmic, and mortals are mortal. When our life is over, we are not, even the best of us, transfigured and taken up into the realm of the cosmics.

Upon visiting the cosmic realm with the ghost, this was quite sadly clear to me. It was plain to see that human beings were so far below the perfection of that realm that it would be utterly impossible for even the most righteous of us to come anywhere near qualifying for that sort of hereafter. As a first thought, I began to wonder if the purpose of that vision was to promote a better understanding of the meaning of grace. But as it turns out, I've learned that grace is only wishful thinking, and worse—a destructive concept that supports our religiously-learned bad habit of wasting the wonderful life that we've been so generously given.

That was the take-home message of that whole indigo ghost episode. The other realm is the domain of immortal spirits, the cosmics. Earth is the domain of us mortal humans. By virtue of the cosmics' tinkering, we have been endowed with mind capabilities that make us far superior to any of the other animals, and even somewhat cosmic-like. In our foolish pride we elevate ourselves to the presumption that someday we'll become truly like them.

But we have but one life, and the opportunity to make of it whatever we will. It is foolish to joylessly and lovelessly waste all of our days through faith in some system of delayed gratification, believing in a glorious outcome that is never going to happen.

After a lifetime of indoctrination, it was difficult for me to give up that belief, even while embracing the idea that the real purpose of life is merely *joy*. *Forsaken* did not seem like the best choice of words for the truth which Bill was insisting that I accept—that I should let go of the notion of immortality. But then I realized that he was expressing it in a way that, from my Christian upbringing, I would surely be able to understand.

There would be no hereafter—for me, or anyone else.

※

11
But What About Bill?

I did wonder about Bill from time to time, whether he was, in fact, the spirit of my long-departed uncle, little Willie Kelderhouse. He was only a little over a year and a half old when he died. How could a toddler have gained the wisdom and supernatural skills of this incorporeal conscience serving as my guardian and guide? Until now, I'd been willing to accept the idea that somehow he had, that I would eventually find out how, and in the meantime I didn't need to worry about that trivial detail. I was sure that there were all sorts of things I didn't know about these entities and their realm, and perhaps never would.

But now I had been told that human beings are never raised up into that domain; that mortals never become immortal. If that was true, then Bill was obviously not the spirit of little Willie. This was a conundrum that perplexed me for a long time.

Bill finally chose to reveal the simple answer: he was not the spirit of little Willie. He was, instead, the *cosmic companion* of the little boy up until the moment of his untimely death!

Forty-one years later I came into the world, and he decided to adopt me as his next charge. That seemed unbelievably coincidental, until I began rethinking the circumstances of my birth.

I had been conceived on South Manitou Island; about seven miles offshore in Lake Michigan from the Kelderhouse farm at Port Oneida. In earlier times, women on the island were delivered by midwives, but by the time of my coming into the world, the island had seen its best days, with most of the younger people having left, and with no women remaining with midwifery skills. As my mother's time approached, my grandfather took her across the passage to the mainland in his trusty mail boat, the Lenore. There she could await the moment of my coming in the comfort of the home where she was born, on the Kelderhouse farm, only a half-hour or so from Traverse City's Munson Hospital, rather than remaining on the island and risking the possibility of inclement weather on the day when the inevitable crossing would become absolutely necessary.

Thus I was, in fact, born in Munson Hospital. After that happy event my mother returned to the farm with her newly born boy, where she stayed temporarily with her mother, brother and sister-in-law until the weather permitted Grandpa Warner to make the crossing again, taking her back home to the island in the calm seas of a pleasant fall day.

That evidently explained how and when Bill and I had become acquainted. I don't know where these cosmic entities dwell; that is, whether they remain in or around a particular location, or whether they're free to roam the entire universe. But in this case at least, the one who came to me, and I came to know as "Bill," was either hanging around the Kelderhouse farm, or just happened to be there for some reason just before or immediately after my birth.

I suspect that Willie meant something to him; that he was attached to the boy and regretted his premature loss. That also explained my affinity to little Willie's burial place in the Kelderhouse cemetery. Perhaps it was his love for the lost boy that brought him back to Port Oneida every now and then, resulting in my very good luck at the moment of our first encounter. Perhaps it was he and I together who somehow felt comforted sitting on the ground during warm summer afternoons at the lost boy's little headstone.

As I realized that these cosmics can have that sort of love for us, I was overwhelmed with feeling. For these beings, so wizened and powerful beyond our poor estate, to value us and love us to this extent in spite of how flawed we are is an overwhelmingly wonderful revelation!

It is a fact after all; no matter what's going on in our lives, someone up there *really does* love us!

———

In the second, and final of these last two appearances, Bill informed me that his time as my cosmic companion was over; that from that point forward, I would be on my own. This was early in my seventy-second year.

I have not yet figured out exactly what that meant. I presumed at the time that it meant that I was very close to the end of my life, but I'm still here, a year later. And I am not actually alone.

Whereas my contact with the cosmics was, up to that point, exclusively with Bill, there are now others, he apparently with them. Sometimes they're attentive, and sometimes not. It's somewhat like being with a group of other adults at a social gathering, where one cannot be the center of attention all the time. Sometimes they respond to requests, making asked-for things happen, seemingly as a whim. From their larger perspective, these asked-for things are probably never considered to be very important. And quite often they do not, never giving any explanation why, but probably for the same reason; that what I might think is urgent or important really isn't.

During any lifetime, everyone must go through all sorts of trials, troubles, sadness, and dangers, and most of us spend the better part of our best years worrying about these things. Some of us eventually realize that somehow we always muddle through, always coming out on the other side into a better day.

During the first decades of life we mostly all also struggle with self-esteem issues, being obsessed with the desire to "be somebody" and make something of ourselves, never realizing that in the eyes of the cosmics, we already are, and will forever be, highly valued and loved unconditionally. Sometimes we are lucky enough to learn this before the final curtain, and can die with the joyous and peaceful feeling of having had a full, sufficiently rewarding life.

Perhaps there is a time when we have become older and wiser, to the extent that our life-long cosmic companion feels able to let go of our hand, trusting that we are finally capable of making the most of whatever time we have left, and admiring us lovingly for what we have become—a "job well done."

❦

12
Belief in Things Not Seen

Who has seen the wind?
    Neither you nor I.
But when the trees bow down their heads,
    The wind is passing by.
Christina Rossetti

"Believe? I cannot believe. I do not believe just for the sake of believing. One must have a reason for a certain hypothesis. When there are sufficient reasons to form a certain hypothesis, I shall accept these reasons, obviously. Then I say, 'We have to accept the possibility of ... whatever'."
Carl Jung

When asked, just before his death in 1961, if he believed in God, Carl Jung's reply was rather lengthy and profound:

"I could not say I believe; I know! I have had the experience of being gripped by something that is stronger than myself, something that people call God."

When he was about thirty-seven, Jung began to occasionally sense a presence—as if he were not alone. Up to this point, although he'd had a falling out with his former friend and colleague, the eminent psychiatrist Sigmund Freud, Jung was still highly regarded. As his ventures into the paranormal became more frequent and profound however, many began to regard him as a crackpot. His most frequent "visitor" took the form of an elderly and very wise man, an apparition he eventually named *Philemon*. Here is what Jung had to say during an interview about these episodes:

> "Philemon and other figures of my fantasies brought home to me the crucial insight that there are things in the psyche which I do not produce, but which produce themselves and have their own life. Philemon represented a force which was not myself. In my fantasies I held conversations with him, and he said things which I had not consciously thought. For I observed clearly that it was he who spoke, and not I.
>
> Psychologically, Philemon represented superior insight. All my works, all my creative activity, has come from those initial fantasies and dreams, which began in 1912. He was a mysterious figure to me. At times he seemed to me quite real, as if he were a living personality. I went walking up and down the garden with him, and to me he was what the Indians call a *guru*.
>
> That religious experiences exist no longer needs proof. But it will always remain doubtful whether

what metaphysics and theology call "God" and the gods is the real ground of these experiences. The question is idle, actually, and answers itself by reason of the subjectively overwhelming numinosity [supernatural nature] of the experience. Anyone who has had it, is seized by it and therefore not in a position to indulge in fruitless metaphysical or epistemological speculations. Absolute certainty brings its own evidence and has no need of anthropomorphic proofs [the attribution of human motivation, characteristics, or behavior to God].

I find my God in my dreams."

Jung thought he had discovered a hidden aspect of the mind, which he called the *collective unconscious*. This peculiar aspect of the mind contained "a reservoir of the experiences of our species,"—fundamental knowledge and universal truths which direct a person's conscious thinking and behavior by means of "archetypes" [a pattern of thought or symbolic imagery,] dreams, and intuition. He came to believe that it was something that every human already possessed as they came into this world, a part of their being which was as common and essential to the whole person as any physical part of their body.

Unfortunately, the collective unconscious contained not only knowledge of good, but also of evil. Furthermore, he thought that this faculty was not confined to space and time, that it was capable of psychic phenomena—producing visions of the future, receiving messages from spirit guides, and such things. Therefore, it seemed to him that the psyche [one's spirit or soul], being not subject to the dimensions of time and space like the physical body, exists in some other realm about which we know nothing.

In Jung's view, this was the manifestation of God, as we know it, and this god exists within every human being. With this understanding in mind, he suggested:

> "Man's relation to God probably has to undergo a certain important change. Instead of the propitiating praise to an unpredictable king, or the child's prayer to a loving father, the responsible living and fulfilling of the divine will in us will be our form of worship and commerce with God."

Near the end of his life, Jung felt quite certain that the *evil* aspect of the collective unconscious, which he had by then renamed the *objective psyche*, would soon prove to be our undoing. At first, he foresaw the total destruction of creation, as we know it here on Earth. But prior to his death, he was evidently led to understand that our world would indeed suffer a terrible calamity, but would not be totally destroyed. Limited areas would escape total annihilation. He shared these dark thoughts only with his closest friends and colleagues. For everyone else, he offered this:

> "As far as we can discern, the sole purpose of human existence is to kindle a light of meaning in the darkness of mere being. God's goodness means grace and light, and his dark side, the terrible temptation of power.

Man has already received so much knowledge that he can destroy his own planet. Nothing shows more drastically than this possibility, how much of divine power has come within the reach of man.

We are the origin of all coming evil. Let us hope that God's good spirit will guide him in his decisions, because it will depend upon man's decisions whether God's creations will continue."

Modern psychology has moved well beyond many of the ideas Jung and Freud came up with in the early years. I, for instance, do not accept the proposition that we are born into this life with a canned archive representing all of the experiences of our species up to the point of our birth. I think it is easy to see how much of what we consider to be fundamental knowledge and universal truths is simply common sense; knowledge passed along from one generation to another, some of it perhaps genetically, and the rest in the normal course of upbringing.

Modern people have lots of different concepts of God—breathtakingly different, as you can see from what Jung, a widely acknowledged genius, thought. Because of the way he conceived of God, Jung had absolutely no doubt that God exists. He could say quite honestly and earnestly, "I do not *believe*—I *know*!"

God made man in his image? More likely, it was the other way around. We typically picture god as a father image—a wise and all-powerful old man with white hair, a full beard, wearing a white robe, possibly with fire shooting out of the tip of his right hand's index finger. Others have dramatically different ideas.

Were you able to get your mind around Jung's concept of God as an intangible and mystical presence in your own mind; a presence that is not confined by the laws of physics, therefore giving you access to, and making you accessible to, metaphysical realms and agents not of this physical world?

That actually makes more sense than the image of God as "father." Jung found the concept acceptable because his visions and dreams provided certain evidence to support such a hypothesis, whereas there is no evidence whatsoever to support the familiar imagery of God being physically and psychologically similar to human beings—save for the brief and highly parsable comment in Genesis 1:26, "And God said, Let us make man in our image, after our likeness ..." In fact, Jung's ideas in this regard were not radically unorthodox, being similar to what many Bible scholars and commentators outside his field of analytical psychology already thought.

Carl Gustav Jung was a religious man. His father, with whom he was quite close during his boyhood, was a pastor in the Swiss Reformed Church who observed a strictly traditional understanding of the faith, as most people did in that time and place. It is therefore not really remarkable that Jung saw the human psyche as "by nature religious," made this religiousness the focus of his explorations, and interpreted most of the experiences described above from a "God" perspective.

However, Jung also allowed for the possibility that his God existed in some form much different than most envisioned—that contrary to the usual understanding of Genesis 1:26, man may, in fact, have created god in *his* own image.

I asserted in the opening pages of this book that it was not a book about religion. Nevertheless, it is a book about *belief*. Humans have always, as far as we know, had some sense of the supernatural, believing that some sort of cosmic consciousness is responsible for, and oversees, the earthly realm within which they live. These beliefs, whether pagan, multi-theistic, monotheistic, or whatever, are always nebulous and vaguely held, as aptly reflected in the Bible passage, "... faith is the assurance of things hoped for, the conviction of things not seen" (Hebrews 11:1). Nevertheless, as each such belief is more elaborately developed over time, it accumulates its dogmas, eventually reaching the point where its believers and proponents are willing to boldly assert that theirs is *the one true religion*—never mind the lack of solid physical evidence.

This is not generally from ignorance, or mindlessly bigoted thinking. It arises from the fact that people have experiences such as I have written about in the preceding pages. In the beginning, someone groping to make sense of such experiences devises an explanation that seems sufficiently plausible. As others encounter similar experiences, they may choose to adopt the same explanation. Over time, a belief system is thus developed and expanded. Earnest and well-meaning as such developments may be, they are invariably flawed to the extent that they attempt the impossible—to describe the indescribable cosmic realm and its supernatural entities in familiar human concepts and terms.

Religions thus established and presently having the largest followings are Christianity, Islam, Hinduism and Buddhism, in that order. To the extent that these are all legitimate attempts to understand the cosmic realm and the entities therein, they can all be respected and honored as steps towards achieving that end.

But these offer only a very simplistic model for understanding the cosmics and their realm, explaining it all in a single three-letter word ... "God." This *God* concept is wholly illogical, but under the rules, cannot be disputed. That serves as a barrier to thinking and the development of a more expansive, intelligent ... and *believable* ... hypothesis.

Only about one out of every five people claim to have experienced some sort of encounter with nonphysical entities from some other realm, with the result that they believe that such entities are real and that another such realm does indeed exists. The majority—the other 80% of the population—has not, and mostly does not. But just as the popular acceptance of a belief does not prove that it is valid, the scant presence of less conventional thinking does not prove it to be false.

Everyone has some sort of religious faith, or lack thereof, and even the most avid practitioner usually has no real basis for what they've come to believe except for peer pressure, either from the family they were born into, or people they associated with thereafter. It's not unusual for people to cling to such beliefs even after they've come to realize that there is no tangible evidence supporting such ideas—so long as available alternatives are similarly nebulous.

Formal education in our modern cultures teaches us to accept that seeing is believing; that if science is not able to prove the reality of something, then it must not exist. That places us logically in the position of not believing in something about which we have no knowledge, and no personal experience, a mindset that is not unlike belief.

But spiritual experiences, such as those described herein, bring with them the overpowering sense of clarity that makes belief, and change, inescapable.

———

Is it really so hard to believe in things unseen?

Place an ice cube, which is merely a small chunk of frozen water, in a pan on the stove. As its hydrogen and oxygen atoms absorb energy in the form of heat, it changes state from solid to liquid, and then again from liquid to vapor, and finally from visible vapor to invisible gas. It is then unseen, but it is still present. If the process is reversed by chilling the gas, it returns to vapor (fog), liquid (water,) and finally back to a solid (ice.) Thanks to science, we now understand how this works, but we've only understood for a few hundred years. Before that, although the physics was exactly the same, the understandings were the subject of speculation and magical beliefs.

We live in the midst of all sorts of invisible intelligence—the electromagnetic waves of radio, television and cellular telephones. This unseen energy carries all sorts of words and pictures, but with modulation schemes and frequencies that our minds are not capable of detecting and deciphering. We therefore need special appliances to focus on a particular signal of interest within this cacophony and convert it to visible images and/or sound more compatible with our own sensory equipment; our ears and our eyes. Is it so difficult to believe that there is probably some sort of modulation and frequency that our minds might be able to decipher without the need of such external conversion? Science has clearly demonstrated that as our mind works, our brain generates electromagnetic waves not unlike these. Just as electronic sensors and instruments are now able to detect, measure and display this energy, we might very well someday find ourselves communicating with each other telepathically via these signals.

The sun shines brightly and gives us light and warmth. It also gives up neutrinos, ghostlike high-energy particles suspected to be almost free of mass, and probably the smallest of all the elemental particles. Hold your palm up between your eyes and the sun for one second, and it will be penetrated by about a billion of these particles, and they readily pass right through it. In fact, they continue on, passing right through your head and even the planet itself, exiting on the opposite side of Earth. Many of these come from far beyond the sun, having been generated by unknown cataclysms in the farthest reaches of the universe. Have you ever heard of such a thing? During your lifetime thus far, believe it or not, an unquantifiable number of these particles have passed unnoticed through your body, and are continuing to do so at this very moment as you read this page. They are not theoretical. Scientists can prove to you that neutrinos are a form of matter that is indeed real. Is it therefore so impossible to entertain the possibility of an unseen form of cosmic consciousness being in your presence throughout your lifetime—the ones I'm calling *the cosmics*?

In considering the nature of these unseen beings, we naturally tend to extrapolate our own, familiar form onto them, envisioning forms that are invisible, but otherwise human-like, similar to us in size and all other respects. Much of this arises because of what we have been conditioned to believe about our having a life after death; "going to heaven," in other words. It has always seemed to me that if such a thing is true, after all these millions of years, heaven must be a very crowded place indeed!

But what do we really know even of ourselves? The highly magnified views of recent brain studies seem to show a sort of lattice structure, with minute strands intersecting each other in three dimensions, the combined length of which probably exceeds 100,000 miles—long enough to circle the globe four times! The purpose of this structure has yet to be figured out, but is thought to involve memory, and it is estimated that the ordinary human brain has a memory capacity sufficient to store the contents of all the books ever printed in the entire world!

Does size really matter? It is quite possible, even quite likely, that the cosmics are invisible for the same reason that sub-atomic particles like the neutrino are invisible—because of their infinitely small size, and the fact that they are, for all practical purposes, composed of energy.

Even if you choose to continue in the belief that when you die you will go to heaven, there is nothing to suggest that you will arrive there in your present physical form, or something like it. Your whole immortal being might be wrapped up in a package no larger than the head of a pin, or even the size of the neutrinos, which are magnitudes smaller.

By the same kind of thinking, there is no reason to think that the cosmics are human-like. They may be very much like the neutrinos—myriad legions freely roaming the universe, and capable of doing so at speeds greater even than the speed of light.

13
The Nature of the Invisibles

In the *Introduction* for this book, I wrote about the dilemma of how to refer to these supernatural entities, and decided, for lack of any better choice, to settle on *cosmics*.

It did occur to me to simply ask them what they call themselves. The answer was this: they don't have an answer, because in their realm there is no language. Nor is there any need for individual identities.

This seems strange and difficult to comprehend from our human perspective. But it really makes perfect sense.

We are able to make sounds because we have the physical apparatus—namely lungs, vocal chords, and an oral cavity—physical attributes which give us that capability. We also have the physical capability of sensing sound. Over the eons of our existence, we have learned how to use our capability of making audible noises to communicate with each other, developing very complex assortments and combinations of sounds, each of which has a particular agreed upon meaning. We call these assortments of sounds *languages*. We learn to use our languages as one means of expressing what's going on in our minds—information about our ideas and feelings.

As we do, another faculty diminishes—the ability to communicate silently by somehow perceiving what another mind is thinking. But that inherent capability never disappears altogether.

When I was a little boy, I communicated that way with the invisible "Bill." After over thirty-six years of marriage and living together, my wife and I are often able to *know* what the other is thinking without expressing it verbally, and often simultaneously blurt out the same thought, as though our minds are linked and operating in concert. Animals do not speak, yet are able to communicate with each other, and even with us. Our cat and I communicate using, for lack of a less hackneyed term, *mental telepathy*. When his food and water dishes need attention, or when he wants to go outdoors, he comes to wherever I am, sits, and stares at me. I am usually able to sense his presence and, upon then paying attention to him, to tell which of these two needs he has on his mind. Everyone has had these sorts of experiences.

The cosmics communicate in this same way among themselves, and with us. There are an estimated 6,500 spoken languages in our physical world. Even the most multi-lingual persons are usually fluent in only two or three. The cosmics are fluent in none of them.

Spoken languages are a tool that allows human beings to be disingenuous. Perhaps that is why they have supplanted our innate means of direct mental communication. But cosmics cannot be fooled. Who has not observed a politician evade a question they didn't want to answer honestly by "spinning" or resorting to "talking points," and readily sensed that they were disingenuously attempting to avoid an inconvenient answer? While religious fundamentalists try to impress each other by "speaking in tongues" or uttering ostentatious prayers, the cosmics would understand this only according to what was going on in the noise-maker's mind; a foolishly arrogant desire to impress their religious peers.

In my very brief visit to the cosmics' realm in the company of the "indigo ghost," I learned that there was no dishonesty there. It didn't occur to me at the time, but the reason for that now seems quite obvious. How could there be? Where the only means of communication is mind-to-mind, perfidy would be impossible.

But quite beyond that, I witnessed that perfection existed in every other context also; that the cosmic realm was totally devoid of *sin*, as we call all of our human vices. Here again, that seemed profoundly miraculous at the time, but after a little thought, it also became readily understandable.

All of our human vices arise from our physical nature. It is said that we appraise each other according to the *three A's*—attractiveness, affluence, and achievement—being envious of another's "looks" and "stuff," in other words, and jealous of another's achievement as the asset that provides easier access to better looks and more stuff. In the non-physical realm of the cosmics, there are no "looks" to envy, no "stuff" to accumulate, and therefore there is no basis for vice. That, in turn, obviates the need of any sort of social organization or regulation, so there is no hierarchical structure of power or influence. The cosmics are not differentiated in any way.

All this frees the cosmic realm up to abide quietly in perfect peace, and limitless joy and love.

Having grown up in a Christian culture, this was not in accord with what I'd been taught—that there is a heaven, with a judgmental God at its head, Jesus at his side, then a hierarchy of adoring saints and angels at their feet. This flawed understanding results from the imposing of our human paradigms on the cosmic realm.

To the extent that there is no hierarchy or division among these cosmic entities, what we perceive as a realm of individual beings can also be thought of collectively as a single omniscient, omnipresent, entity ... like "god." But there is no supreme being, no demigods, no saints, nor any higher or lower-ranking angels.

I eventually learned this from the cosmics themselves—that they prevail all over our universe, and that these equal entities, acting corporately in our lives, are what humans have always interpreted as the gods, or God.

14
The Origin of Mind

So what about "creation?" Who or what did it, and for what purpose?

There are all sorts of legends and speculations about the origin of the universe and mankind. The legends are found mostly in religious traditions. The speculations are philosophical or scientific—or perhaps we should say pseudo-philosophical and pseudo-scientific.

We are all familiar with the religious traditions, most of which are archaic and simplistic creation legends. In attempts to explain away the logical flaws in these stories—for instance; "If god created everything, where did god come from?" or again, "If prior to creation there was nothing, how could there have been a creator god?"—writers employ all sorts of obscure philosophical and/or scientific contrivances. The attempted explanations are never successful; at least not to a thinking person.

The same is true of philosophical and scientific attempts to answer these questions. We are led into discussions about what the dimension of *time* is, and how time exists in the universe only with respect to its origin at the moment of the *big bang*—that before that space was a timeless void. The religious inference in this is an entity forever existing as a universal and infinite mind in a timeless and unquantifiable domain.

Then again, some theorize that the universe is oscillatory, big bangs producing epochs of expansion to near infinite size and then, upon reaching its kinetic limits it reverses in epochs of contraction, which produces infinitesimally tiny packets of infinite mass and energy, culminating in another big bang—thus producing serial epochs of creation and annihilation, each having its own new time dimension.

The universe is unimaginably large—essentially infinite, from our perspective. At the same time a complementarily tiny sub-atomic "universe" also exists. Thanks to scientific instruments developed by our best minds at great expense (e.g., radio telescope arrays, the Hubble and Kepler deep space observatories, the Large Hadron Collider, etc.,) we have learned a lot about both, but very little about either with respect to what there probably is to know. Each discovery reveals even deeper mysteries.

Creation and the purpose of life? These are truly frequently asked questions. They reflect our inquisitive nature; a human attribute that serves mankind well, if only by reason of making life more interesting. But, on the other hand, they clearly reveal our penchant for preoccupying ourselves with things that do not matter. Short of being told directly by the cosmics, we cannot know these things. They are unknowable, and probably forever will be, because we have no need of knowing them.

What need have we to know whether or not some sort of life exists on some far distant body in the universe? From what we have already learned, scientists speculate that habitable planets probably average about sixty light-years (5.9-trillion miles) apart and civilizations about 2,000 light-years apart. If true, it would obviously be far beyond our capability of travel and communication. Our life spans are so short compared to the time required even for electromagnetic signals traveling near the speed of light to traverse the intervening distances, that any information exchanged would be far outdated and of little practical value, except for initially confirming the existence of intelligent life elsewhere in the universe—which we can already rather safely assume to be the case, given the infinite possibilities currently existing in the vastness of space.

What about the development of intelligent life on Earth in particular, and the origin of life in a more immediate sense; the birth of a human child, and the development of its mind?

The emergence of the Earth as a planet capable of developing and sustaining any sort of life, at least as we know it, resulted from an improbable combination of astrophysical and geological events and circumstances. Speculations to the contrary notwithstanding, few, if any, other planets with prospectively similar histories have thus far actually been found to exist anywhere in the universe.

At present, scientists place the age of Earth at about 4.5-billion years. During that time, life is thought to have evolved through a complex sequence of events and biochemical processes. Not much happened for the first 4-billion years, during which only very simple life forms appeared—bacteria, plankton, and algae. Then about 550-million years ago, and for reasons science can presently only speculate about, there occurred a series of much more rapid developments. Over the next hundreds of millions of years, these resulted in the gradual appearance of more complex creatures, which became the ancestors of almost all presently existing animal life, including humans.

Somewhere during this process, the cosmics took notice of this unique place in the universe, finding human-like prototypes among the array of evolving life forms. Intrigued with what was happening here, they decided to meddle with what was naturally developing, perhaps merely out of idle curiosity, singling out one very interesting life form—one which walked upright—as a candidate for *intellect*.

This was the origin of *mind*, the thing that distinguishes human beings from all the other animals, and led to their dominance of life on Earth. It became a very interesting experiment for the cosmic observers, but one with unintended and unfortunate consequences.

⚜

15
From Mind to Madness

Egocentric as we are, our contemplations of creation are always apt to center on *life* and the origin thereof, as if that is the most important and profoundly complex part of it. But is life really any more extraordinary than any other aspect of creation?

Consider the rocks—from Mauna Kea, the greatest monolithic pile, to the lowliest grain of sand.

A typical grain of sand consists mainly of silicon dioxide, which is represented by the chemical symbol "SiO_2" signifying a molecule consisting of one silicon atom joined to two oxygen atoms. A single grain of sand contains some 26,000,000,000,000,000,000 such molecules, or a total of 78,000,000,000,000,000,000 (78-quintillion) atoms. Silicon atoms have fourteen electrons; oxygen atoms have eight. These orbit the nucleus of the atom they belong to, which contains an equal number of protons, some neutrons, and various other minor particles. The 78-quintillion silicon and oxygen atoms in the grain of sand are held tightly together in a precise lattice structure by virtue of an orderly swapping system involving their outer shell orbital electrons. Although the grain of sand seems inert, the orbiting of its 1.7-sextillion electrons is a manifestation of the orderly activity going on within, and the energy involved. The electron bonds are so tight, that a lot of energy is required to disturb its structure by any external means—a bolt of lightning, for example, which occasionally turns individual grains of sand into *fulgurites*; delicate glass shapes sometimes called "petrified lightning."

This is a much simplified analysis of a grain of sand, but even at this level, it is rather awe inspiring to realize that even this tiny and relatively insignificant bit of matter is a busy place, and one of astounding structural complexity. How did such a thing evolve? Where did silicon and oxygen atoms come from in the first place, and what prompted their bonding to create the rock that over millions of years was ground down by the forces of nature into the innumerable grains of golden sand we so much enjoy at our beaches on warm summer days?

The next time you're at the beach, observe a single grain of its sand on the tip of your index finger, contemplate all that's going on inside, and appreciate how even a grain of sand is, in fact, a remarkable creation!

Our realm is full of all sorts of remarkable creations. Mineral, vegetable or animal, they are all made up of combinations of elementary particles and energy spewed forth from the cosmos to combine in vast assortments of configurations and activity levels. Some, like the rocks, are seemingly eternal. Others are more short-lived, although in a larger sense the seemingly short-lived are often not that at all since, unlike the rocks, they have a means of reproducing themselves, and often in quantity! These are what we think of as *life*.

We are life, and although perhaps the most robust manifestation of it, yet we are merely part of creation's myriad array of accomplishments.

What makes humans special is not the evolution of the very complex physical bodies we inhabit, but rather, something that came as a gift from the cosmic realm—*mind*.

Endowing us with cosmic-like intellectual capabilities did indeed change our role as a part of what was developing on Earth in profound and very interesting ways. We rapidly became superior to and dominant over all other forms of life. But what the cosmics had not anticipated was that in us, because we have a physical form, it would also result in the development of *consciousness, a sense of emotional sensitivity, and self awareness* and that would lead to all sorts of unhappy consequences.

Being non-physical themselves, the cosmics could probably not have anticipated this.

———

Archaeology dates our ancestry back as far as six million years; however recent evidence suggests that a divergence occurred about 4.1-million years ago between what became bipedal hominids and what branched off as our closest relatives, the knuckle-walking chimpanzees. It is tempting to speculate that this was the moment when the cosmics stepped in, and that is what prompted this profound change in one particular strain of the chimp family.

However, it is also true that the intellectual capabilities of our early ancestors developed very slowly. For most of these millions of years they lived off the land; hunting, fishing and gathering—this combination of activities, in itself, distinguishing humanoids from all other animals. Then sometime between ten and twenty thousand years ago our ancestors began to develop agrarian skills, it apparently having finally occurred to them that domesticating certain plants and animals was a good way to ensure a reliable source of sustenance without having to roam thither and yon from one season to the next. Strangely, this most significant single development in human history is known to have happened simultaneously in widely separated areas of the earth!

How could that have occurred in an age so far predating any means of intercontinental communication and travel?

Early humans were resourceful, but not very creative, employing sticks and rocks as tools and animal skins as clothing. That also changed about this same time, as artisans and craftsmen began to make all sorts of useful things out of clay and metal, while others also became artistically creative—turning figments of their imagination into physical form, just for the pleasure of passing time doing so.

Was *this* perhaps the point when the cosmics stepped in—only ten or twenty thousand years back in our history? Or was it possibly their second intervention?

Humans accomplished many remarkable things during the intervening millennia between then and the past few centuries, nevertheless all of it put together rates a poor second to what has been achieved since the advent of the mid-eighteenth century's *Industrial Revolution*, thanks mainly to the development of formal systems of education and training—the passing on of acquired knowledge from one generation to the next.

These epochs of long term quiescence culminating in inexplicable instances of sudden cultural and technological advancement, suggest that the cosmics did not intervene in human evolution just one time. Perhaps we are merely their playthings. There is nothing in this history of humanity's development that suggests any sort of master plan, and not everything about these cosmic interventions has turned out to be for our betterment.

The cosmic-given intellect that has led to our continuing advancement has also enabled our transition as creatures that have constantly become progressively more dangerous. Among all the amazing and wonderfully useful things that we have created, we have also developed meanness, and devised all sorts of ways to hurt each other, even to the extent of inventing and perfecting a means of totally destroying the very world we live in.

16
The Mystery of Human Wickedness

Mind is not the same thing as *brain*. It's always tempting to compare the brain to today's much simpler personal computers, but the comparison is appropriate only in the most elementary sense.

Like the computer, the brain has processing and memory capabilities, but they are not provided by discretely identifiable components as in a computer. In fact, nobody actually knows exactly how the brain processes information and stores memories, those functions appearing to be distributed over widely diverse areas. Like a computer, the brain also has inputs and outputs; the inputs being the five senses, and the outputs being speech and motor control signals that operate muscles and produce physical movements of the body. Also like the computer, part of the brain's processing power is used by the central nervous system, which regulates the so called *autonomic* body functions. The rest of it is available to *thinking*.

Dr Suzana Herculano-Houzel, a researcher in Brazil, has recently determined that the adult male brain is made up of about 86,000,000,000 neurons (100-billion was previously estimated and is often cited.) That's about thirteen times more brain cells than are found in our closest relative, the common chimpanzee. Neurons are specialized, impulse-conducting cells consisting of the cell body itself and its input/output connectors, the axon and dendrites. These are interconnected to form a massive biochemical system that communicates neuron-to-neuron by means of low level electrical impulses.

The much larger size of the human brain suggests that there must be a lot more going on there than in the very similar, but very much smaller brains of all the other animals. And, in fact, there is.

Animal behavior is usually attributed mostly to *instinct*, with only minimal learning capabilities after that. Instinct is often thought of as a hard wired set of behaviors peculiar to each animal type and as something that animals are mysteriously born with. Humans similarly have what appears to be a commonly inherited set of shared ideas and behaviors which provides us with a fundamental ability to thrive in our environment and get along with each other. Carl Jung called this an *objective psyche*, but was not able to determine its seemingly mysterious source. You will soon see that this is not so mysterious after all.

In the meantime, we already commonly understand that genes determine our physical characteristics and certain behavioral traits. Over the millions of years that we've been around, we've had plenty of time to develop a package of basic behavioral information that can be passed on through the reproductive process by means of DNA. But this is mostly about physical behavior—crying when unhappy, smiling and laughing when pleased, turning our attention to the source of unfamiliar noises, our *fight or flight responses*, and so on. It is not about intellectual mind functions.

If each new person had to learn these fundamentals from scratch, there would be very little, if any, human progress on account of the chaos that would certainly prevail. And so, in addition to code that enables the brain to properly operate the various autonomic body functions and essential physical behaviors, we are somehow imbued with some information about values and behavioral standards. Unlike animal instincts, these fundamental ideas, attitudes and behavior patterns are apt to subsequently be modified by *cognitive processes.*

As we proceed through life, very little of what we experience is lost to the mind, whether we're conscious of it or not. As each new situation is encountered or observed, it is subconsciously compared to information already in memory to determine its nature, meaning and relevance, before being inserted into our ever expanding array of remembered information. This is the cognitive process. Our attitudes and behaviors at any given time in life are the result of all the cognitive processing that has gone on up to that point; the nature of all the inputs, how that information was accumulated into arrays of seemingly related material, and how it influenced subsequent cognitive tasks.

With this in mind, it is easy to see how no two people confronted with the same situation would interpret it and react to it in exactly the same way. The only way that might come close to happening would be for identical twins to be brought up in a tightly cloistered environment, such that, like the fictional Tweedledum and Tweedledee, their observations and life experiences were also virtually identical.

This might seem like a remarkably ingenious system ... until you consider the impact of bad data. Since the mind is imperfect, the cognitive process is quite apt to generate incorrect or inappropriate determinations of the nature, meaning and relevance of any particular observance or event.

As a very simple example, you might consciously or subconsciously overhear someone claim that all foreigners are bad. If you are a child having little or no preexisting information with which to process that information and interpret it more intelligently, it'll go into memory as a valid fact about *foreigners*, rather than being marked as an invalid generalization and the narrow minded opinion of just one person. As time goes on, future cognitive processing having anything to do with foreigners will then be colored by that bad data, thereby being stored away as yet another incorrect or inappropriate cognition. If permitted to continue without some sort of intervention, you would wind up being a hopelessly xenophobic adult, even to the point of being able to kill foreigners without hesitation or remorse.

The great power of the human mind derives from its ability to do some very sophisticated cognitive processing. By *thinking recursively*, we can develop new ideas from previously existing information by reprocessing it over and over again, perfecting or altering it in some way with each successive pass. By *combinatorial thinking* we are able to develop new ideas by combining separate previously existing cognitions—sometimes even widely disparate and seemingly unrelated ideas.

Our mind uses abstract *mental symbols* to organize information, store and retrieve memories, and to create, link, and extend categories of cognitions and memories. Its thousands of mental symbols are highly organized with each one representing one of many objects and abstract concepts that we have, at some time or another, thought about ... vehicles, furniture, the future, our hopes, good, evil, pets, pain, friends, and even ourselves.

Think about "school" for a moment ... *school* being a label that we are using here; not the symbol itself, since symbols exist only in the abstract domain. This will *bring to mind*, as it were, an encyclopedic review of every bit of information your mind has in its memory having to do with education: teachers, schools, school buildings, school rooms, school books, fellow students, and on and on, seemingly *ad infinitum*. The longer you permit your mind to dwell on it, the further it will delve down into this mental label and all those linked to it.

Now stop, and realize that all that information is organized in your mind under a single top-level mental label. Thus whenever you are confronted with some new information related to this subject, this mental label will be called up as part of the cognitive process and all this existing information will determine what your mind's perception of the new information will be.

The mind is also capable of *abstraction*—"thinking outside the box"—to conceptualize, generalize, and to see patterns and meanings beyond the obvious and use those ideas or clues to solve problems in novel and unexpected ways. When combined with the other processes—recursive and combinatorial thinking plus mental images—the result can often be highly imaginative, revolutionary or inventive!

But, to get back to the point, there is nothing in the nature of *mind* that guarantees accuracy or restricts these marvelous functions to positive purposes. Thus all human thinking is fallible, and probably always will be, and that fallibility is the explanation for the *mystery of human wickedness.*

People are never born accursed, nor are they ever born blessed. Human behavior is the result of a learning process, and like all other things in nature, is arrayed along a standard distribution from minus to plus, bad to good, evil to virtuous, wicked to kind, or whatever. Obviously, that learning process is highly influenced by the circumstances a person is born into, but the mind's cognitive processing continues to work until the moment of death, enabling it to modify its view of the outside world, and adjust its behavior accordingly. Thus we understand the mind's potential for corruption, but also the possibility of its reformation.

There is no Satan, nor are there any *errant cosmics* to scapegoat for human error and wickedness. We are the origin of our own attitudes and behavior.

17
The Cosmics' Role in Your Life

At the moment of our birth, or shortly thereafter, most of us are chosen by one of these cosmic friends. That particular cosmic becomes our life-long companion, our *cosmic companion*. The coming of this cosmic companion is the beginning of *mind* in every human being, and the origin of *conscience*. It is therefore also the beginning of our *humanity*. Here is the answer to the conundrum in today's debates over women's reproductive rights: when does a fetus become a *person*?

It is also the answer to Jung's question about the origin of what he called the collective unconscious, and later, the objective psyche; this reservoir of fundamental knowledge and universal truths which direct our conscious thinking and behavior. It comes with the arrival of our cosmic companion, not as instinct, or as code in our DNA.

As infants, our brains are not sufficiently developed such that we have any awareness of this sudden presence. During early childhood, many of us become acquainted with this imaginary friend, but as our intellectual abilities continue to develop and we are enrolled in structured intellectual educational activities, we are taught about *reality* and learn that what is truly *real* is limited to that which can be verified by physical evidence. Our awareness of our ever-present cosmic companion then fades away, sometimes never to return.

Our cosmic companion has a role in protecting us from physical harm, regulating our behavior, and influencing our decision-making, but does not ordinarily interfere with free will. In my experience, however, my cosmic companion has occasionally intervened on its own to prevent my death or to prevent me from going through with some neurotically-driven self-destructive behavior. It has also sometimes offered unsolicited advice and counseling when I was troubled. Nevertheless, this sort of support ordinarily comes only when it *is* asked for. And when it *is* solicited, it is usually quickly forthcoming.

Thinking about these things, clearly we are not always protected from physical harm since people obviously do often die of other than natural causes, including suicide. They also often make bad decisions which cost them dearly in terms of love, reputation or wealth. So one might wonder exactly what role this cosmic companion does play in our lives, whether it can and will sometimes protect us from harm, what prompts its unsolicited interventions, and so on.

The answers are simple enough, although possibly mundane to the extent of being a disappointment to some who would like to believe in cosmic miracle workers.

The cosmics are wise and companionate mentors who are always at our side, teaching and counseling. They are not magicians. They have no power to miraculously heal or physically intervene in order to prevent catastrophes.

If we are in the midst of making decisions that are apt to have unpleasant consequences, they may choose to become involved by causing us to slow down and give the matter more thought, or to think about it in some new way. But they never make decisions for us. Moreover, we are not obligated to submit to their counseling or to accept their advice. Very often we do not, and then suffer the consequences. Here then is the answer to another conundrum: the question religious people often ask about why bad things happen to good people.

For example, a nominally *good person* has dinner and a few drinks with his wife and some close friends. He is aware that the few before-dinner cocktails and after-dinner cordials have elevated his blood alcohol level, but lets his pride overrule his better judgment (his cosmic companion's gentle reminder) and he refuses to let a sober designated driver do the driving on the way back home. Swerving to avoid a small animal, the car catches the shoulder of the road and careens across the median of the highway and into the path of an oncoming semi-trailer truck. His wife is killed instantly, and he spends the rest of his life in a wheelchair and with his regrets. How could such a thing happen to such a nice couple!

We humans are all fallible, even the best of us. Our cosmic companions can urgently intervene with reminders, advice and even warnings, but they cannot force us to listen. Nor can they take physical control of a skidding vehicle in order to prevent a tragedy that appears imminent as the result of our refusal to accept their infallible counseling.

All religions have stories about how god, or the gods, intervened in human affairs to cause a certain outcome, and such tales arise even in everyday life. The outcome of such narratives usually favor the original teller of the story, be it about a military victory, a ball game won, or even some more pedestrian thing. Setting aside miracles such as the legendary parting of the red sea, the rest can be understood as instances where those involved listened to the superior wisdom of the cosmics and then acted advisedly. The good outcomes were affected by human agencies, in other words, not by any miraculous intervention of a deity who favored one side over another. Quite likely, the losing side was the one that chose not to seek such counseling or ignored that which had been given.

Right does not always make might, nor does it always win out in the end. There are plenty of stories, in history and real life, about heroes being subdued by supposedly villainous forces; Israel being subdued by the Philistines, for example, or the home team loosing out to a traditional rival. Nothing guarantees that the cosmics of the favored side will prevail over those of the other side. The fact is that the favored side is just a matter of perspective; it's usually the side that we're on, or the one that wrote the history. When it so happens that the other side comes out on top, it's not because their *evil* cosmics are more powerful, but probably because they asked for guidance, listened carefully, and acted accordingly.

Miraculous healing is another magical power that is often boasted of in religion, but is not within the capabilities of the cosmics. On the other hand, disease and crippling conditions resulting from nervous or psychological causes are not unknown. One only need study the scientific data regarding the *placebo effect* to understand that people are often as healthy, or as ill or disabled, as they think they are.

For example, it was recently revealed through the publishing of FDA test data that the six leading antidepressant drugs are no more effective in relieving depression than sugar pills, or, said the other way around, placebos were found to be just as effective in relieving depression as the six leading antidepressant drugs the FDA examined.

Lest we jump to the conclusion that millions of people have been and are being ripped off to the tune of billions of dollars on medicines that owe their popularity as much to marketing as to chemistry, consider that the placebos worked only because people thought that they were getting a widely accepted and highly expensive miracle drug. To that extent, the pharmaceutical companies can be credited with the cures!

With this in mind, is it so hard to believe that Jesus of the Bible story was able to restore the sight of Bartimaeus, a man who apparently believed that Jesus was a demigod; the promised messiah? Interestingly, upon restoring his sight, Jesus of Nazareth supposedly uttered, "Go; your faith has healed you." The traditional understanding is, of course, one of a healing miracle proving that Jesus had god-like powers. It is more plausible that Jesus meant what he said, that the blind man's sight cleared up because he believed unquestionably in that possibility; in other words, because of the placebo effect.

Modern day evangelists also often claim to have healing powers and, in fact, to the extent that they can make themselves believable, they probably oftentimes do.

In this manner, the cosmics can, and do, promote healing, by enabling the person who is suffering some injury or disease to truly believe that they can recover. But that can only work when the disorder is caused by, or notably influenced by, emotional or psychological factors. Magic cannot mend a broken leg, and cancer obviously cannot be cured by the power of mind over matter. When spontaneous (miraculous) cures seem to have happened, the likely reality is that the original diagnosis was incorrect. That is not at all unusual; it happens about 20% of the time according to medical studies, including reviews of autopsies.

This will give you some idea of what you can expect of your cosmic companion and the other cosmics over the course of your life. If up to this point in your life you have been a magical thinker and a believer in miracles, there have no doubt been many occasions where that did not work out well. Instead of continuing on that path, consider taking complete responsibility for your life, and then listen carefully for those still, small voices that have always been at your side, and are still ready, willing and able to offer their guidance and protection.

18
Still Small Voices

It might sometimes seem that the cosmics are not interested in personal relationships with us mortals. From what has been presented in the previous pages, it should be obvious that this is by no means the case. We can communicate with them, and they with us.

When I originally heard comedian, satirist (and agnostic) Bill Maher joke that prayer was "an attempt to communicate telepathically with an imaginary being," I thought that was very cleverly humorous, and committed that line to memory. But it has since occurred to me that the act of praying might not be so ridiculous after all. Setting aside the simplistic idea of "talking to God," mental telepathy, or some similar phenomenon, is the medium of communication used by the cosmics, among themselves, and with us.

Prayer, in ordinary religious practice, is usually a monologue rather than a conversation. One merely voices his or her confessions, concerns, petitions, or whatever, with the faith that someone is listening, and not expecting any sort of immediate acknowledgment. This is not descriptive of our commerce with the cosmics, so the concept of prayer, as it is typically understood in religious contexts, does not apply.

So just how do we communicate with the cosmics?

If, as a small child, you ever had an "imaginary" friend, then you already know or, at least did once know, the answer. It wasn't something you had to learn, or practice; it just came naturally—so naturally, in fact, that it never occurred to you to wonder where they came from, or when, or why they were invisible to everyone else. You merely established a psychic link with that entity, and conversations ensued; two way conversations.

Unfortunately, as we grow up, we are taught to use our mind for purposes deemed by the culture to be more constructive and productive. Our educational system is focused on logical thinking, analysis, and accuracy, while our parental upbringing most often teaches us that aesthetics, feelings, and creativity have few practical applications in the conduct of our daily lives. We are taught much about language, and how to use it correctly to communicate concisely. Daydreaming is condemned as a waste of time.

As we move into our adult years, we become consumed with the tasks of career development, and the responsibilities and obligations of supporting ourselves and our own growing families. Ultimately we find ourselves with a mind that is highly capable in logical, sequential, rational, analytical, and objective operations, but severely atrophied in its ability to do random, intuitive, holistic, synthesizing, and subjective sorts of thinking. This actually becomes a handicap, because in fact, these two kinds of thinking actually augment each other. Highly effective people have minds that are both analytical and imaginative.

It is not possible to undo years of learning and mind development. It is also not easy to learn how to turn off all the noise in your mind arising from the practical concerns and challenges of adult life. However, with practice, it is possible to recover much of your childlike ability of communicating with the cosmics.

This is where you might suspect the discussion to turn to meditation or hypnosis. But as a child you obviously knew nothing about such things. When talking with your imaginary friends, you were sometimes surely daydreaming. But more often you were just earnestly involved in whatever sort of play the two or more of you ordinarily enjoyed.

The cosmics are always around you and accessible to you. If you have some desire to communicate with them, you merely need to clear your mind, concentrate on your side of the conversation, and listen with your mind for the responses. You don't need to make a big deal of this by doing it in a trance-like séance setting, in a particular place, or at any particular time.

But it's hard to listen to still, small voices when your mind is preoccupied with the noise of all your day-to-day concerns. It will probably take some practice for you to learn how to momentarily set all that aside and clear your mind so that it can become receptive to telepathic communications.

Furthermore, there might not always be a response from the cosmics' realm just because you decide that you wish to talk. Maybe you actually have nothing to talk about, are just testing, or are otherwise bringing up things not considered worthy of or necessitating any response.

This doesn't mean that your commerce with the cosmics need always involve deeply troubling or perplexing issues. It wasn't that way when you were a child, was it? The cosmics love you, and would enjoy merely having a conversational relationship with you.

Just as any of your mortal friends will quickly tire of your constant complaining and awfulizing, so it is with your cosmic friends, who more than your mortal friends will surely realize that such misery is mostly of your own making. If you have a problem or a special need, do indeed talk about it, but don't ask for or expect any miracles. The cosmics do not have miracle making capabilities, but they can direct your thinking, and that of others, into channels that will prove productive of happy outcomes.

Once you learn (or re-learn) the skill of communicating with the cosmics, you will realize that they have been speaking to you all along, but you just interpreted their inputs as ideas of your own making, rather than recognizing their true source.

You will also eventually develop a feeling for their constant presence and the depth of their affection, after which you will never again feel alone.

19
Living with the Cosmics

In the foregoing, parallels with various religions are obvious. That has not been intentional, but is unavoidable.

What is *religion* anyway?

"... a set of beliefs concerning the cause, nature, and purpose of the universe, especially when considered as the creation of a superhuman agency or agencies, usually involving devotional and ritual observances, and often containing a moral code governing the conduct of human affairs."

From that dictionary point of view, perhaps this could be considered a religious text of sorts. But my purpose is merely to share my experience and tell about what it taught me, not to support, or debunk, any established faith. My experience supports the first half of this definition, but not the last half—the part about devotional and ritual observances and moral codes.

They taught me that we are intellectually the creation of cosmic entities, but they are so far superior that our worship of them or their realm would be totally meaningless to them, and is uncalled for. What need might they possibly have in their state of perfection, to be corporately, ritualistically, and unceasingly praised by the likes of us?

Our continuing need for affirmation commonly arises out of our human self-esteem issues, and this we innocently, but misguidedly, confer upon the cosmic realm, where such issues have never existed. There is no such need, and our offering of *worship* is therefore no doubt seen as naively misguided, and probably even pathetic.

We are loved unconditionally by these cosmic entities, which have made us what we are. It is a love much deeper than we are ordinarily capable of. It is unconditional because in the cosmic realm there is no alternative. It is nonjudgmental because the criteria we use in judging each other have no relevance in that realm, and therefore no commerce. In the absence of judgment, confessions and pleas for forgiveness are also pointless and inappropriate.

It is sufficient for us to return that love through responsible and joyful living and the fulfilling of the good that their interventions intended for us. After coming to understand our relationship to them, that is a very easy thing to do. That understanding is a very personal thing that happens spontaneously, not something we can be taught as institutionalized religious dogma or theology. It cannot be taught; it must be experienced. Anyone who is touched by one of these entities will know beyond any doubt what that sort of love is all about without needing any other kind of instruction.

It can be yours to receive, and yours to give. You need only open your mind to the possibility.

www.ingramcontent.com/pod-product-compliance
Lightning Source LLC
Chambersburg PA
CBHW020657300426
44112CB00007B/412